Creed or Chaos?

A Forthright Edition™

Sophia Institute Press awards the privileged title "A Forthright Edition" to a select few of our books that address contemporary Catholic issues with clarity, cogency, and force, and that are also destined to become classics for all times.

> Forthright Editions are *direct*, explaining their principles briefly, simply, and clearly to Catholics in the pews, on whom the future of the Church depends. The time for ambiguity or confusion is past.

> Forthright Editions are *contemporary*, born of our own time and circumstances and intended to become significant voices in current debates, voices that serious Catholics cannot ignore, regardless of their prior views.

> Forthright Editions are *classical*, addressing themes and enunciating principles that are valid for all ages and cultures. Readers will turn to them time and again for guidance in other days and different circumstances.

> Forthright Editions are *charitable*, entering contemporary debates solely in order to clarify basic issues and to demonstrate how those issues can be resolved in a way that strengthens souls and the Church.

Please feel free to suggest topics and authors for future Forthright Editions. And please pray that Forthright Editions may help to resolve the crisis of the Church in our day.

Dorothy L. Sayers

Creed or Chaos?

Why Christians Must Choose
Either Dogma or Disaster
(Or, Why It Really Does
Matter What You Believe)

SOPHIA INSTITUTE PRESS®
Manchester, New Hampshire

The first American edition of *Creed or Chaos?* was published in 1949 in New York by Harcourt, Brace. Sophia Institute Press published a hardcover edition in 1995 and a paperback edition in 1996. This 1999 Forthright Edition by Sophia Institute Press includes a new subtitle and a new format.

Jacket design by Lorraine Bilodeau

The cover artwork is a montage of *Chartres Cathedral* (Corbis / Craig Aurness) and *Forest Fire Consuming Tree* (Corbis / Jeff Vanuga).

Sophia Institute Press®
Box 5284, Manchester, NH 03108
1-800-888-9344
www. sophiainstitute.com

Library of Congress Cataloging-in-Publication Data

The Library of Congress has cataloged an earlier version of this work as follows:

Sayers, Dorothy L. (Dorothy Leigh), 1893-1957.
  Creed or chaos? / Dorothy L. Sayers.
        p. cm.
  Originally published: New York : Harcourt, Brace, c1949.
  ISBN 0-918477-27-1
  ISBN 0-918477-31-X (pbk.)
  1. Theology, Doctrinal. I. Title.
BT 15.S3   1995
230 — dc20   95-8261   CIP

99 00 01 02 03 9 8 7 6 5 4 3 2 1

Contents

❧

Foreword
by John L. Barger

More than twenty-five years ago, my late wife, Susan, read the introduction to Dorothy Sayers's translation of Dante's *Divine Comedy*. A non-Christian at the time, Susan was struck by Sayers's forceful insistence that the *Divine Comedy* can only be understood as "the drama of the soul's choice" between good and evil, revealing "the terror and splendor of Christian Revelation."[1] Susan later said that, in an instant, these words made sense not only of the *Comedy*, but of the sorrows and tragedies that she — like most of the rest of us — had been suffering incomprehensibly until then.

Sayers's words prompted Susan to reconsider the claims of Christianity and finally to embrace that God and His Church so dramatically depicted in the *Divine Comedy*.

[1] *The Comedy of Dante Alighieri the Florentine*: *Cantica I*, *Hell (L'Inferno)*, trans. Dorothy L. Sayers (New York: Penguin Books Ltd., 1949), 11.

Creed or Chaos?

A few years later, thanks to Susan (and to Dorothy Sayers), I, too, was received into the Roman Catholic Church. We will not be the last pilgrims won to Roman Catholicism by the uncompromising voice of Dorothy Sayers, whose eloquent defense of doctrine remains unmatched to this day.

Sadly, although Sayers played a key role in our own conversions (and that of many others), she herself never entered the Church whose doctrines she so bravely defended. This is so despite the fact that, as one of her biographers notes, she had a thorough grasp of the teachings of the Roman Catholic Church and accepted *all* of its tenets except its rejection of the validity of Anglican orders and its assertion of papal supremacy.[2] The *New Catholic Encyclopedia* echoes this point: "On practically every point of theology, her orthodoxy was unimpeachable."[3]

Later in these pages, you will encounter Sayers's bold defense of the central importance of doctrine to faith:

> "Take away theology and give us some nice religion" has been a popular slogan for so long that we are apt to accept it, without inquiring whether religion

[2] James Brabazon, *Dorothy L. Sayers: A Biography* (New York: Avon Books, 1981), 69.

[3] *The New Catholic Encyclopedia*, s.v. "Sayers, Dorothy Leigh."

without theology has any meaning. . . . The reason why the Churches are discredited today is not that they are too bigoted about theology, but that they have run away from theology. The Church of Rome alone has retained Her prestige because She puts theology in the foreground of Her teaching.

These are words rarely heard from any pulpit today, Roman Catholic or not, yet their acceptance is essential if the Faith is to grow strong again. For that reason, they need to be heard — along with the reasons behind them — by all men and women of good will who seek to live in accordance with the teachings of Christ.

Let us, then — Catholics and non-Catholics alike — be grateful that Dorothy Sayers had the skill and the grace and the will to proclaim this truth loudly, clearly, and persuasively to all mankind; and that we now have the privilege of publishing these words for a new generation of readers who may have forgotten (if they ever knew) that *there can be no true religion without doctrine*.

However, a warning: Dorothy Sayers's remaining just outside the Catholic Church colors some of her terminol·ogy. Thus, for example, she does not use the expression "the Church" to refer simply or solely to the Roman Catholic Church (or to any other institutional church);

rather, she speaks broadly of "the Church" as that body of believers who profess one of the traditional, official Creeds of Christianity: the Apostles' Creed, the Nicene Creed, and so forth.

Similarly, when Sayers criticizes "the Church" for failing to preach the doctrines found in the Creeds, her target is not any particular denomination, but rather the weak or confused pastors of her day — leaders in all denominations — who watered down the Creeds to make them more palatable to their contemporaries.

Because this diluting tendency has only grown worse — not better — since these pages were written, you'll surely be familiar with the mindless answers to catechetical questions that Sayers satirizes in "The Dogma is the Drama." (But after you've laughed, ask yourself whether your own knowledge of the Creed is really any better.)

It's not an idle question, as you'll soon come to see. As Dorothy Sayers demonstrates, the Creed — that precisely formulated and clearly defined set of Christian beliefs — is our only defense against chaos. As far as time, talent, and circumstances allow, you and I need to master the Creed: the teachings of Christ as they are found in His own words as recorded in the Gospels and in the formal, dogmatic teachings of His Church. If you are not convinced of this, these pages will show you why.

However, before you plunge into these engaging pages, a few words about the text may be helpful. First, most of the essays in this book were originally composed at the height of World War II. Hence, when Dorothy Sayers refers to "the Germans," she usually has in mind the Nazi leaders and their ideology, rather than the German people themselves.

Second, as an extremely literate person, Dorothy Sayers laced these essays with quotations from authors and works both modern and classical, but only rarely identified their sources. We have tracked down and footnoted the source of most of these quotations and have supplied translations for the occasional British slang expressions whose meaning may not be obvious to modern American readers.

Yes, you'll encounter slang in these pages; for although religion is serious business, Dorothy Sayers never lets it become ponderous. Delicate readers, be forewarned: here is strong meat indeed: criticisms levelled with uncompromising force and rapier accuracy, rhetorical flourishes that bring to mind the dashing finesse of the Three Musketeers, with whom Sayers was enthralled in her adolescence.

Indeed, Dorothy Sayers is a swashbuckling apologist, a devoted knight ever questing to defend the honor of

Lady Doctrine with all the weapons at her disposal. If sometimes she exaggerates the ferocity of the dragons she attacks, this only serves to make their slaying more delightful.

Nor is this a disservice to truth: if sometimes Dorothy Sayers overstates her case at the beginning of a paragraph, be patient, attentive, and forgiving: by its end, she always moderates and qualifies her points so deftly that Truth shines forth the brighter — brighter because of the strong contrast created by her earlier, rhetorical claims.

May that bright Truth now embrace her tenderly, and may it embrace you, too, as you read on!

❧

Creed or Chaos?

Chapter One

⸎

The Greatest Drama Ever Staged

is the official Creed of Christendom

Official Christianity, of late years, has been having what is known as "a bad press." We are constantly assured that the churches are empty because preachers insist too much upon doctrine — "dull dogma," as people call it. The fact is the precise opposite. It is the neglect of dogma that makes for dullness. The Christian faith is the most exciting drama that ever staggered the imagination of man — and the dogma *is* the drama.

That drama is summarized quite clearly in the Creeds of the Church,[4] and if we think it dull, it is because we either have never really read those amazing documents, or have recited them so often and so mechanically as to have lost all sense of their meaning. The plot pivots upon a single character, and the whole action is the answer to a single central problem: *What think ye of Christ?*

[4] The Apostles' Creed, the Nicene Creed, and the Athanasian Creed follow the biographical note in this book.

Creed or Chaos?

Before we adopt any of the unofficial solutions (some of which are indeed excessively dull), before we dismiss Christ as a myth, an idealist, a demagogue, a liar, or a lunatic, it will do no harm to find out what the Creeds really say about Him. What does the Church think of Christ?

The Church's answer is categorical and uncompromising, and it is this: That Jesus Bar-Joseph, the carpenter of Nazareth, was in fact and in truth, and in the most exact and literal sense of the words, the God *"by whom all things were made."* His body and brain were those of a common man; His personality was the personality of God, so far as that personality could be expressed in human terms. He was not a kind of demon or fairy pretending to be human; He was in every respect a genuine living man. He was not merely a man so good as to be "like God" — He *was* God.

Now, this is not just a pious commonplace; it is not commonplace at all. For what it means is this, among other things: that for whatever reason God chose to make man as he is — limited and suffering and subject to sorrows and death — He had the honesty and the courage to take His own medicine. Whatever game He is playing with His creation, He has kept His own rules and played fair. He can exact nothing from man that He has not exacted from Himself. He has Himself gone through the whole of human experience, from the trivial irritations of family life and the cramping restrictions of hard work and lack of money to the worst horrors of pain and humiliation, defeat, despair, and death. When He was a man, He played the man. He was born in poverty and died in disgrace and thought it well worthwhile.

Christianity is, of course, not the only religion that has found the best explanation of human life in the idea of an incarnate and suffering god. The Egyptian Osiris died and rose again; Aeschylus in his play, *The Eumenides*, reconciled man to God by the theory of a suffering Zeus. But in most theologies, the god is supposed to have suffered and died in some remote and mythical period of prehistory.

The Christian story, on the other hand, starts off briskly in St. Matthew's account with a place and a date: "When Jesus was born in Bethlehem of Judea in the days of Herod the King."[5] St. Luke, still more practically and prosaically, pins the thing down by a reference to a piece of government finance. God, he says, was made man in the year when Caesar Augustus was taking a census in connection with a scheme of taxation.[6] Similarly, we might date an event by saying that it took place in the year that Great Britain went off the gold standard. About thirty-three

[5] Matt. 2:1 (King James Version).
[6] Luke 2:1.

years later (we are informed) God was executed, for being a political nuisance, *"under Pontius Pilate"* — much as
we might say, "when Mr. Joynson-Hicks was Home Sec-
retary." It is as definite and concrete as all that.

Possibly we might prefer not to take this tale too
seriously — there are disquieting points about it. Here
we had a man of Divine character walking and talking
among us — and what did we find to do with Him? The
common people, indeed, "heard Him gladly,"[7] but our
leading authorities in Church and State considered that
He talked too much and uttered too many disconcerting
truths. So we bribed one of His friends to hand Him over
quietly to the police, and we tried Him on a rather vague
charge of creating a disturbance, and had Him publicly
flogged and hanged on the common gallows, "thanking
God we were rid of a knave."[8] All this was not very cred-
itable to us, even if He was (as many people thought and
think) only a harmless crazy preacher. But if the Church
is right about Him, it was more discreditable still; for the
man we hanged was God Almighty.

So that is the outline of the official story — the tale
of the time when God was the underdog and got beaten,

[7] Mark 12:37.

[8] Cf. William Shakespeare, *Much Ado About Nothing*, Act
3, scene 3, lines 29-30.

when He submitted to the conditions He had laid down and became a man like the men He had made, and the men He had made broke Him and killed Him. This is the dogma we find so dull — this terrifying drama of which God is the victim and hero.

If this is dull, then what, in Heaven's name, is worthy to be called exciting? The people who hanged Christ never, to do them justice, accused Him of being a bore; on the contrary, they thought Him too dynamic to be safe. It has been left for later generations to muffle up that shattering personality and surround Him with an atmosphere of tedium. We have very efficiently pared the claws of the Lion of Judah, certified Him "meek and mild," and recommended Him as a fitting household pet for pale curates and pious old ladies.

To those who knew Him, however, He in no way suggested a milk-and-water person; *they* objected to Him as a dangerous firebrand. True, He was tender to the unfortunate, patient with honest inquirers, and humble before Heaven; but He insulted respectable clergymen by calling them hypocrites; He referred to King Herod as "that fox";[9] He went to parties in disreputable company and was looked upon as a "gluttonous man and a wine-bibber,

---

[9] Luke 13:32.

a friend of publicans and sinners";[10] He assaulted indignant tradesmen and threw them and their belongings out of the Temple; He drove a coach-and-horses through a number of sacrosanct and hoary regulations; He cured diseases by any means that came handy, with a shocking casualness in the matter of other people's pigs and property; He showed no proper deference for wealth or social position; when confronted with neat dialectical traps, He displayed a paradoxical humor that affronted serious-minded people, and He retorted by asking disagreeably searching questions that could not be answered by rule of thumb.

He was emphatically not a dull man in His human lifetime, and if He was God, there can be nothing dull about God either. But He had "a daily beauty in His life that made us ugly,"[11] and officialdom felt that the established order of things would be more secure without Him. So they did away with God in the name of peace and quietness.

"*And the third day He rose again*": what are we to make of that? One thing is certain: if He was God and nothing else, His immortality means nothing to us; if He was man

[10] Matt. 11:19.
[11] Cf. William Shakespeare, *Othello*, Act 5, scene 1, lines 19-20.

and no more, His death is no more important than yours
or mine. But if He really was both God and man, then
when the man Jesus died, God died too, and when the
God Jesus rose from the dead, man rose too, because they
were one and the same person.

The Church binds us to no theory about the exact
composition of Christ's Resurrection Body. A body of
some kind there had to be, since man cannot perceive
the Infinite otherwise than in terms of space and time. It
may have been made from the same elements as the body
that disappeared so strangely from the guarded tomb, but
it was not that old, limited, mortal body, though it was
recognizably like it. In any case, those who saw the risen
Christ remained persuaded that life was worth living and
death a triviality — an attitude curiously unlike that of
the modern defeatist, who is firmly persuaded that life is
a disaster and death (rather inconsistently) a major
catastrophe.

Now, nobody is compelled to believe a single word
of this remarkable story. God (says the Church) has created us perfectly free to disbelieve in Him as much as we
choose. If we do disbelieve, then He and we must take
the consequences in a world ruled by cause and effect.
The Church says further that man did, in fact, disbelieve,
and that God did, in fact, take the consequences. All the

same, if we are going to disbelieve a thing, it seems on the whole to be desirable that we should first find out what, exactly, we are disbelieving. Very well, then: "*The right Faith is: that we believe and confess that our Lord Jesus Christ . . . is God and Man . . . perfect God and perfect Man, of a reasonable soul and human flesh subsisting. . . . Who although He be God and Man, yet is He not two, but one Christ.*"[12] There is the essential doctrine, of which the whole elaborate structure of Christian faith and morals is only the logical consequence.

Now, we may call that doctrine exhilarating or we may call it devastating; we may call it Revelation or we may call it rubbish; but if we call it dull, then words have no meaning at all. That God should play the tyrant over man is a dismal story of unrelieved oppression; that man should play the tyrant over man is the usual dreary record of human futility; but that man should play the tyrant over God and find Him a better man than himself is an astonishing drama indeed. Any journalist, hearing of it for the first time, would recognize it as News; those who did hear it for the first time actually called it News, and good news at that; though we are apt to forget that the word *Gospel* ever meant anything so sensational.

[12] The Athanasian Creed.

The Greatest Drama Ever Staged

Perhaps the drama is played out now, and Jesus is safely dead and buried. Perhaps. It is ironical and entertaining to consider that once at least in the world's history those words might have been spoken with complete conviction, and that was upon the eve of the Resurrection.

Chapter Two

⁓

The Triumph of Easter

※

"O *felix culpa!*" said Augustine of Hippo, rather dangerously, with reference to the sin of Adam. "O happy guilt, that did deserve such and so great a Redeemer!"[13]

It is difficult, perhaps, to imagine a pronouncement that lays itself more open to misunderstanding. It is the kind of paradox that bishops and clergy are warned to beware of uttering from the pulpit. But, then, the Bishop of Hippo was a very remarkable bishop indeed, with a courage of his convictions rare in highly placed ecclesiastical persons.

If spiritual pastors are to refrain from saying anything that might ever, by any possibility, be misunderstood by anybody, they will end — as in fact many of them do — by never saying anything worth hearing. Incidentally, this particular brand of timidity is the besetting sin of the

---

[13] The *Exsultet* in the Liturgy for Holy Saturday.

good churchman. Not that the Church approves it. She knows it of old for a part of the great, sprawling, drowsy, deadly sin of Sloth — a sin from which the preachers of fads, schisms, heresies, and anti-Christ are most laudably free.

The children of this world are not only (as Christ so caustically observed) wiser in their generation than the children of light;[14] they are also more energetic, more stimulating and bolder. It is always, of course, more amusing to attack than to defend; but good Christian people should have learnt by now that it is best to defend by attacking, seeing that "the Kingdom of Heaven suffereth violence, and the violent take it by force."[15]

St. Augustine, anyway, seeing the perpetual problem of sin and evil being brought up and planted, like a battery, against the Christian position, sallied promptly forth, like the good strategist he was, and spiked its guns with a thanksgiving.

The problem of sin and evil is, as everybody knows, one which all religions have to face, especially those that postulate an all-good and all-powerful God. "If," we say readily, "God is holy and omnipotent, He would interfere

[14] Luke 16:8.
[15] Matt. 11:12.

and stop all this kind of thing" — meaning by "this kind of thing" wars, persecutions, cruelty, Hitlerism, Bolshevism, or whatever large issue happens to be distressing our minds at the time. But let us be quite sure that we have really considered the problem in all its aspects.

"Why doesn't God smite this dictator dead?" is a question a little remote from us. Why, madam, did He not strike you dumb and imbecile before you uttered that baseless and unkind slander the day before yesterday? Or me, before I behaved with such cruel lack of consideration to that well-meaning friend? And why, sir, did He not cause your hand to rot off at the wrist before you signed your name to that dirty little bit of financial trickery?

You did not quite mean that? But why not? Your misdeeds and mine are nonetheless repellent because our opportunities for doing damage are less spectacular than those of some other people. Do you suggest that your doings and mine are too trivial for God to bother about? That cuts both ways; for, in that case, it would make precious little difference to His creation if He wiped us both out tomorrow.

Well, perhaps that is not quite what we meant. We meant why did God create His universe on these lines at all? Why did He not make us mere puppets, incapable of executing anything but His own pattern of perfection? Some schools of thought assert that He did, that everything we do (including Jew baiting in Germany and our own disgusting rudeness to Aunt Eliza) is rigidly determined for us, and that, however much we may dislike the pattern, we can do nothing about it. This is one of those theories that are supposed to free us from the trammels of superstition. It certainly relieves our minds of all responsibility; unfortunately, it imposes a fresh set of trammels of its own. Also, however much we may believe in it, we seem forced to behave as though we did not.

Christians (surprising as it may appear) are not the only people who fail to act up to their creed; for what determinist philosopher, when his breakfast bacon is uneatable, will not blame the free will of the cook, like any Christian? To be sure, the philosopher's protest, like his bacon, is predetermined also; that is the silly part of it. Our minds are the material we have to work upon when constructing philosophies, and it seems but an illogical creed, whose proof depends on our discarding all the available evidence.

The Church, at any rate, says that man's will is free, and that evil is the price we pay for knowledge, particularly the kind of knowledge which we call self-consciousness.

It follows that we can, by God's grace, do something about the pattern. Moreover, God Himself, says the Church, is doing something about it — with our cooperation, if we choose, in spite of us if we refuse to cooperate — but always, steadily, working the pattern out.

And here we come up against the ultimate question which no theology, no philosophy, no theory of the universe has ever so much as attempted to answer completely. Why should God, if there is a God, create anything, at any time, of any kind at all? That is a real mystery, and probably the only completely insoluble mystery there is. The one person who might be able to give some sort of guess at the answer is the creative artist, and he, of all people in the world, is the least inclined even to ask the question, since he is accustomed to take all creative activity as its own sufficient justification.

But we may all, perhaps, allow that it is easier to believe the universe to have come into existence for some reason than for no reason at all. The Church asserts that there is a Mind which made the universe, that He made it because He is the sort of Mind that takes pleasure in creation, and that if we want to know what the Mind of the Creator is, we must look at Christ. In Him, we shall discover a Mind that loved His own creation so completely that He became part of it, suffered with and for it, and made it a sharer in His own glory and a fellow worker with Himself in the working out of His own design for it.

That is the bold postulate that the Church asks us to accept, adding that, if we do accept it (and every theoretical scheme demands the acceptance of some postulate or other) the answers to all our other problems will be found to make sense.

Accepting the postulate, then, and looking at Christ, what do we find God "doing about" this business of sin and evil? And what is He expecting us to do about it? Here, the Church is clear enough. We find God continually at work turning evil into good.

Not, as a rule, by irrelevant miracles and theatrically effective judgments — Christ was seldom very encouraging to those who demanded signs, or lightnings from Heaven, and God is too subtle and too economical a craftsman to make very much use of those methods. But He takes our sins and errors and turns them into victories, as He made the crime of the Crucifixion to be the salvation of the world. "O *felix culpa!*" exclaimed St. Augustine, contemplating the accomplished work.

Here is the place where we are exceedingly liable to run into misunderstanding. God does not need our sin, still less does He make us sin, in order to demonstrate His power and glory. His is not the uneasy power that has to reassure itself by demonstrations. Nor is it desirable that we should create evils on purpose for the fun of seeing Him put them right. That is not the idea at all. Nor yet are we to imagine that evil does not matter, since God can make it all right in the long run.

Whatever the Church preaches on this point, it is *not* a facile optimism. And it is not the advisability of doing evil that good may come. Oversimplification of this sort is as misleading as too much complication and just as perilously attractive. It is, for instance, startling and illuminating to hear a surgeon say casually, when congratulated upon some miracle of healing, "Of course, we couldn't have done that operation without the experience we gained in the War."

There is a good result of evil; but, even if the number of sufferers healed were to exceed that of all the victims who suffered in the War, does that allay the pangs of the victims or of any one of them, or excuse the guilt that makes war possible? No, says the Church, it does not. If an artist discovers that the experience gained through his worst sins enables him to produce his best work, does that entitle him to live like a beast for the sake of his art? No, says the Church, it does not. We can behave as badly as we like, but we cannot escape the consequences. "Take what you will, said God" (according to the Spanish

proverb), "take it and pay for it." Or somebody else may
do the paying and pay fully, willingly, and magnificently,
but the debt is still ours. "The Son of Man goeth as it is
written of Him; but woe unto that man by whom the Son
of Man is betrayed! It had been good for that man if he
had not been born."[16]

When Judas sinned, Jesus paid; He brought good out
of evil, He led out triumph from the gates of Hell and
brought all mankind out with Him; but the suffering of
Jesus and the sin of Judas remain a reality. God did not
abolish the fact of evil: He transformed it. He did not
stop the Crucifixion: He rose from the dead.

"Then Judas, which had betrayed Him, when he saw
that He was condemned, . . . cast down the pieces of sil-
ver in the temple, and departed, and went and hanged
himself."[17] And thereby Judas committed the final, the
fatal, the most pitiful error of all; for he despaired of God
and himself, and never waited to see the Resurrection.
Had he done so, there would have been an encounter, and
an opportunity, to leave invention bankrupt; but unhap-
pily for himself, he did not. In this world, at any rate, he
never saw the triumph of Christ fulfilled upon him, and

[16] Matt. 26:24.
[17] Matt. 27:3, 5.

through him, and in spite of him. He saw the dreadful payment made, and never knew what victory had been purchased with the price.

All of us, perhaps, are too ready, when our behavior turns out to have appalling consequences, to rush out and hang ourselves. Sometimes we do worse, and show an inclination to go and hang other people. Judas, at least, seems to have blamed nobody but himself, and St. Peter, who had a minor betrayal of his own to weep for, made his act of contrition and waited to see what came next. What came next for St. Peter and the other disciples was the sudden assurance of what God was, and with it the answer to all the riddles.

If Christ could take evil and suffering and do that sort of thing with them, then of course it was all worthwhile, and the triumph of Easter linked up with that strange, triumphant prayer in the Upper Room, which the events of Good Friday had seemed to make so puzzling. As for their own parts in the drama, nothing could now alter the fact that they had been stupid, cowardly, faithless, and in many ways singularly unhelpful; but they did not allow any morbid and egotistical remorse to inhibit their joyful activities in the future.

Now, indeed, they could go out and "do something" about the problem of sin and suffering. They had seen the strong hands of God twist the crown of thorns into a crown of glory, and in hands as strong as that they knew themselves safe. They had misunderstood practically everything Christ had ever said to them, but no matter: the thing made sense at last, and the meaning was far beyond anything they had dreamed. They had expected a walkover, and they beheld a victory; they had expected an earthly Messiah, and they beheld the Soul of Eternity.

It had been said to them of old time, "No man shall look upon My face and live";[18] but for them a means had been found. They had seen the face of the living God turned upon them; and it was the face of a suffering and rejoicing Man.

[18] Exod. 33:20.

Chapter Three

✌

The Dogma Is the Drama

꩜

"Any stigma," said a witty tongue, "will do to beat a dogma"; and the flails of ridicule have been brandished with such energy of late on the threshing floor of controversy that the true seed of the Word has become well-nigh lost amid the whirling of chaff.

Christ, in His Divine innocence, said to the Woman of Samaria, "Ye worship ye know not what"[19] — being apparently under the impression that it might be desirable, on the whole, to know what one was worshipping. He thus showed Himself sadly out of touch with the twentieth-century mind, for the cry today is: "Away with the tedious complexities of dogma — let us have the simple spirit of worship; just worship, no matter of what!" The only drawback to this demand for a generalized and undirected worship is the practical difficulty

[19] John 4:22.

of arousing any sort of enthusiasm for the worship of nothing in particular.

It would not perhaps be altogether surprising if, in this nominally Christian country, where the Creeds are daily recited, there were a number of people who knew all about Christian doctrine and disliked it. It is more startling to discover how many people there are who heartily dislike and despise Christianity without having the faintest notion what it is. If you tell them, they cannot believe you. I do not mean that they cannot believe the doctrine: that would be understandable enough, since it takes some believing. I mean that they simply cannot believe that anything so interesting, so exciting, and so dramatic can be the orthodox Creed of the Church.

That this is really the case was made evident to me by the questions asked me, mostly by young men, about my Canterbury play, *The Zeal of Thy House*.[20] The action of the play involves a dramatic presentation of a few fundamental Christian dogmas — in particular, the application to human affairs of the doctrine of the Incarnation. That the Church believed Christ to be in any *real* sense God, or that the Eternal Word was supposed to be associated in any way with the work of Creation; that Christ was held

[20] Commissioned for the Canterbury festival of 1937.

to be at the same time Man in any *real* sense of the
word; that the doctrine of the Trinity could be considered to have any relation to fact or any bearing on psy-
chological truth; that the Church considered pride to be
sinful, or indeed took notice of any sin beyond the more
disreputable sins of the flesh — all these things were
looked upon as astonishing and revolutionary novelties,
imported into the Faith by the feverish imagination of
a playwright.

I protested in vain against this flattering tribute to
my powers of invention, referring my inquirers to the
Creeds, to the Gospels, and to the offices of the Church;
I insisted that if my play was dramatic it was so, not in
spite of the dogma but because of it — that, in short, the
dogma *was* the drama. The explanation was, however,
not well received; it was felt that if there was anything
attractive in Christian philosophy I must have put it
there myself.

Judging by what my young friends tell me, and also by
what is said on the subject in anti-Christian literature
written by people who ought to have taken a little trouble to find out what they are attacking before attacking
it, I have come to the conclusion that a short examina-
tion paper on the Christian religion might be very generally answered as follows:

Q.: *What does the Church think of God the Father?*

A.: He is omnipotent and holy. He created the world and imposed on man conditions impossible of fulfillment; He is very angry if these are not carried out. He sometimes interferes by means of arbitrary judgments and miracles, distributed with a good deal of favoritism. He likes to be truckled to[21] and is always ready to pounce on anybody who trips up over a difficulty in the Law, or is having a bit of fun. He is rather like a dictator, only larger and more arbitrary.

Q.: *What does the Church think of God the Son?*

A.: He is in some way to be identified with Jesus of Nazareth. It was not His fault that the world was made like this, and, unlike God the Father, He is friendly to man and did His best to reconcile man to God (see *Atonement*). He has a good deal of influence with God, and if you want anything done, it is best to apply to Him.

Q.: *What does the Church think about God the Holy Ghost?*

A.: I don't know exactly. He was never seen or heard of till Pentecost. There is a sin against Him which damns you forever, but nobody knows what it is.

[21] English slang for "to be submitted to slavishly."

Q.: *What is the doctrine of the Trinity?*

A.: "The Father incomprehensible, the Son incomprehensible, and the whole thing incomprehensible." It's something put in by theologians to make it more difficult — it's got nothing to do with daily life or ethics.

Q.: *What was Jesus Christ like in real life?*

A.: He was a good man — so good as to be called the Son of God. He is to be identified in some way with God the Son (see above). He was meek and mild and preached a simple religion of love and pacifism. He had no sense of humor. Anything in the Bible that suggests another side to His character must be an interpolation, or a paradox invented by G. K. Chesterton. If we try to live like Him, God the Father will let us off being damned hereafter and only have us tortured in this life instead.

Q.: *What is meant by the Atonement?*

A.: God wanted to damn everybody, but His vindictive sadism was sated by the crucifixion of His own Son, who was quite innocent, and, therefore, a particularly attractive victim. He now only damns people who don't follow Christ or who never heard of Him.

Q.: *What does the Church think of sex?*

A.: God made it necessary to the machinery of the world, and tolerates it, provided the parties (a) are married, and (b) get no pleasure out of it.

Q.: *What does the Church call Sin?*

A.: Sex (otherwise than as excepted above); getting drunk; saying "damn"; murder, and cruelty to dumb animals; not going to church; most kinds of amusement. "Original sin" means that anything we enjoy doing is wrong.

Q.: *What is faith?*

A.: Resolutely shutting your eyes to scientific fact.

Q.: *What is the human intellect?*

A.: A barrier to faith.

Q.: *What are the seven Christian virtues?*

A.: Respectability; childishness; mental timidity; dullness; sentimentality; censoriousness; and depression of the spirits.

Q.: *Wilt thou be baptized in this Faith?*

A.: No fear!

I cannot help feeling that as a statement of Christian orthodoxy, these replies are inadequate, if not misleading. But I also cannot help feeling that they do fairly accurately represent what many people take Christian orthodoxy to be, and for this state of affairs I am inclined to blame the orthodox.

Whenever an average Christian is represented in a novel or a play, he is pretty sure to be shown practicing one or all of the Seven Deadly Virtues listed above, and I am afraid that this is the impression made by the average Christian upon the world at large.

Perhaps we are not following Christ all the way or in quite the right spirit. We are apt, for example, to be a little sparing of the palms and the hosannas. We are chary of wielding the scourge of small cords, lest we should offend somebody or interfere with trade. We do not furbish up our wits to disentangle knotty questions about Sunday observance and tribute-money, nor hasten to sit at the feet of the doctors, both hearing them and asking them questions. We pass hastily over disquieting jests about making friends with the mammon of unrighteousness and alarming observations about bringing not peace but a sword; nor do we distinguish ourselves by the graciousness with which we sit at meat with publicans and sinners.

Somehow or other, and with the best intentions, we have shown the world the typical Christian in the likeness of a crashing and rather ill-natured bore — and this in the Name of One who assuredly never bored a soul in those thirty-three years during which He passed through this world like a flame.

Let us, in Heaven's name, drag out the Divine Drama from under the dreadful accumulation of slipshod thinking and trashy sentiment heaped upon it, and set it on an open stage to startle the world into some sort of vigorous reaction. If the pious are the first to be shocked, so much the worse for the pious — others will enter the Kingdom of Heaven before them. If all men are offended because of Christ, let them be offended; but where is the sense of their being offended at something that is not Christ and is nothing like Him? We do Him singularly little honor by watering down His personality till it could not offend a fly. Surely it is not the business of the Church to adapt Christ to men, but to adapt men to Christ.

It is the dogma that is the drama — not beautiful phrases, nor comforting sentiments, nor vague aspirations to loving-kindness and uplift, nor the promise of something nice after death — but the terrifying assertion that the same God who made the world lived in the world and passed through the grave and gate of death. Show that to the heathen, and they may not believe it; but at least they may realize that here is something that a man might be glad to believe.

Chapter Four

Creed or Chaos?

"And when he is come, he will reprove the world
of sin, and of righteousness, and of judgment:
of sin, because they believe not on me;
of righteousness, because I go to my Father,
and ye see me no more; of judgment,
because the prince of this world is judged."

John 16:8-11

꒎

Something is happening to us today which has not hap-
pened for a very long time.[22] We are waging a war of
religion. Not a civil war between adherents of the same
religion, but a life-and-death struggle between Christian
and pagan. The Christians are, it must be confessed, not
very good Christians, and the pagans do not officially
proclaim themselves worshippers of Mohammed or even
of Odin, but the stark fact remains that Christendom and
heathendom now stand face-to-face as they have not done
in Europe since the days of Charlemagne. In spite of the
various vague references in sermons and public speeches
to the War as a "crusade," I think we have scarcely begun
to realize the full implications of this.

It is a phenomenon of quite extraordinary importance.
The people who say that this is a war of economics or of

[22] This essay is based on an address delivered at Derby, England, May 4, 1940.

39

power politics, are only dabbling about on the surface of things. Even those who say it is a war to preserve freedom and justice and faith have gone only halfway to the truth. The real question is what economics and politics are to be used for; whether freedom and justice and faith have any right to be considered at all; at bottom it is a violent and irreconcilable quarrel about the nature of God and the nature of man and the ultimate nature of the universe; it is a war of dogma.

The word *dogma* is unpopular, and that is why I have used it. It is our own distrust of dogma that is handicapping us in the struggle. The immense spiritual strength of our opponents lies precisely in the fact that they have fervently embraced, and hold with fanatical fervor, a dogma which is nonetheless a dogma for being called an "ideology." We on our side have been trying for several centuries to uphold a particular standard of ethical values which derives from Christian dogma, while gradually dispensing with the very dogma which is the sole rational foundation for those values. The rulers of Germany have seen quite clearly that dogma and ethics are inextricably bound together. Having renounced the dogma, they have renounced the ethics as well — and from their point of view they are perfectly right. They have adopted an entirely different dogma, whose ethical scheme has no value

for peace or truth, mercy or justice, faith or freedom; and
they see no reason why they should practice a set of virtues incompatible with their dogma.

We have been very slow to understand this. We persist
in thinking that Germany "really" believes those things
to be right that we believe to be right, and is only very
naughty in her behavior. That is a thing we find quite
familiar. We often do wrong things, knowing them to be
wrong. For a long time we kept on imagining that if we
granted certain German demands that seemed fairly reasonable, she would stop being naughty and behave according to our ideas of what was right and proper. We still go
on scolding Germany for disregarding the standard of
European ethics, as though that standard was something
which she still acknowledged. It is only with great difficulty that we can bring ourselves to grasp the fact that
there is no failure in Germany to live up to her own standards of right conduct. It is something much more terrifying and tremendous: it is that what we believe to be evil,
Germany believes to be good. It is a direct repudiation of
the basic Christian dogma on which our Mediterranean
civilization, such as it is, is grounded.

I do not want now to discuss the ideology of Germany,
nor yet that of Russia which, in rather a different way, is
also a repudiation of Christendom. Nor do I want to talk

about our own war aims and peace aims, and how far we are single-minded about them. All I want to say on this point is that, however deeply we have sinned — and God knows we have done plenty of evil in our time — we have not gone so far as to have altogether lost all claim to stand for Christendom. There is a great difference between believing a thing to be right and not doing it, on the one hand, and, on the other, energetically practicing evil in the firm conviction that it is good. In theological language, the one is mortal sin, which is bad enough; the other is the sin against the Holy Ghost, which is without forgiveness simply and solely because the sinner has not the remotest idea that he is sinning at all. So long as we are aware that we are wicked, we are not corrupt beyond all hope. Our present dissatisfaction with ourselves is a good sign. We have only to be careful that we do not get too disheartened and abashed to do anything about it all.

The only reason why I have mentioned Germany is this: that in the present conflict we have before us, in a visible and physical form which we cannot possibly overlook, the final consequences of a quarrel about dogma. A quarrel of that kind can go on for a very long time beneath the surface, and we can ignore it so long as disagreement about dogma is not translated into physical terms. While there is a superficial consensus of opinion

about the ethics of behavior, we can easily persuade ourselves that the underlying dogma is immaterial. We can,
as we cheerfully say, "agree to differ." "Never mind about
theology," we observe in kindly tones, "if we just go on
being brotherly to one another it doesn't matter what we
believe about God." We are so accustomed to this idea
that we are not perturbed by the man who demands: "If
I do not believe in the fatherhood of God, why should I
believe in the brotherhood of man?" That, we think, is
an interesting point of view, but it is only talk — a subject for quiet after-dinner discussion. But if the man goes
on to translate his point of view into action, then, to our
horror and surprise, the foundations of society are violently shaken, the crust of morality that looked so solid
splits apart, and we see that it was only a thin bridge over
an abyss in which two dogmas, incompatible as fire and
water, are seething explosively together.

Now in this assembly I may take it for granted that we
are generally agreed as to what is good and what is evil.
However little we may have lived up to our beliefs, I take
it that we are ready, if challenged, to cry, like the paladins
in *The Song of Roland:* "Pagans are wrong, Christians are
in the right."[23]

---

[23] "*Paiens unt tort e Chrestiens unt dreit.*" *The Song of Roland,*
79, line 1015.

Creed or Chaos?

The thing I am here to say to you is this: that it is worse than useless for Christians to talk about the importance of Christian morality, unless they are prepared to take their stand upon the fundamentals of Christian theology. It is a lie to say that dogma does not matter; it matters enormously. It is fatal to let people suppose that Christianity is only a mode of feeling; it is vitally necessary to insist that it is first and foremost a rational explanation of the universe. It is hopeless to offer Christianity as a vaguely idealistic aspiration of a simple and consoling kind; it is, on the contrary, a hard, tough, exacting, and complex doctrine, steeped in a drastic and uncompromising realism. And it is fatal to imagine that everybody knows quite well what Christianity is and needs only a little encouragement to practice it. The brutal fact is that in this Christian country not one person in a hundred has the faintest notion what the Church teaches about God or man or society or the person of Jesus Christ.

If you think I am exaggerating, ask the Army chaplains. Apart from a possible one percent of intelligent and instructed Christians, there are three kinds of people we have to deal with. There are the frank and open heathen, whose notions of Christianity are a dreadful jumble of rags and tags of Bible anecdote and clotted mythological

nonsense. There are the ignorant Christians, who com-
bine a mild gentle-Jesus sentimentality with vaguely
humanistic ethics — most of these are Arian heretics.[24]
Finally, there are the more or less instructed churchgoers,
who know all the arguments about divorce and auricular
confession and communion in two kinds, but are about
as well equipped to do battle on fundamentals against a
Marxian atheist or a Wellsian agnostic as a boy with a
peashooter facing a fan-fire of machine guns. Theologi-
cally, this country is at present in a state of utter chaos,
established in the name of religious toleration, and rap-
idly degenerating into the flight from reason and the
death of hope. We are not happy in this condition and
there are signs of a very great eagerness, especially among
the younger people, to find a creed to which they can
give wholehearted adherence.

This is the Church's opportunity, if She chooses to
take it. So far as the people's readiness to listen goes,
She has not been in so strong a position for at least two
centuries. The rival philosophies of humanism, enlightened self-interest, and mechanical progress have broken
down badly; the antagonism of science has proved to
be far more apparent than real, and the happy-go-lucky

[24] Or possibly Adoptionists. They do not formulate their
theories with any great precision.

doctrine of *laissez-faire* is completely discredited. But no good whatever will be done by a retreat into personal piety or by mere exhortation to a "recall to prayer." The thing that is in danger is the whole structure of society, and it is necessary to persuade thinking men and women of the vital and intimate connection between the structure of society and the theological doctrines of Christianity.

The task is not made easier by the obstinate refusal of a great body of nominal Christians, both lay and clerical, to face the theological question. "Take away theology and give us some nice religion" has been a popular slogan for so long that we are apt to accept it, without inquiring whether religion without theology has any meaning. And however unpopular I may make myself, I shall and will affirm that the reason why the Churches are discredited today is not that they are too bigoted about theology, but that they have run away from theology. The Church of Rome alone has retained Her prestige because She puts theology in the foreground of Her teaching. Some of us may perhaps think it a rather unimaginative and confined theology; but that is not the point. The point is that the Church of Rome is a theological society, in a sense in which the Church of England, taken as a whole, is not; and that because of this insistence on theology,

She is a body disciplined, honored, and sociologically important.

I should like to do two things this afternoon. First, I would like to point out that if we really want a Christian society we must teach Christianity, and that it is absolutely impossible to teach Christianity without teaching Christian dogma. Secondly, I want to put before you a list of half a dozen or so main doctrinal points which the world most especially needs to have drummed into its ears at this moment — doctrines forgotten or misinterpreted, but which (if they are true as the Church maintains them to be) are cornerstones in that rational structure of human society which is the alternative to world chaos.

I shall begin with this matter of the inevitability of dogma, if Christianity is to be anything more than a little mild wishful thinking about ethical behavior.

Writing the other day in *The Spectator*, Dr. Selbie, former Principal of Mansfield College, discussed the subject of "The Army and the Churches." In the course of this article there occurs a passage that exposes the root cause of the failure of the Churches to influence the life of the common people.

> The rise of the new dogmatism [he says] whether
> in its Calvinist or Thomist form, constitutes a

fresh and serious threat to Christian unity. The tragedy is that *all this, however interesting to theologians, is hopelessly irrelevant to the life and thought of the average man,* who is more puzzled than ever by the disunion of the Churches, as well as by the theological and ecclesiastical differences on which it is based.[25]

Now I am perfectly ready to agree that disputes between the Churches constitute a menace to Christendom. And I will admit that I am not quite sure what is meant by "the new dogmatism"; it might, I suppose, mean the appearance of new dogmas among the followers of St. Thomas and Calvin respectively. But I rather fancy it means a fresh attention to, and reassertion of, old dogma, and that when Dr. Selbie says that "all this" is irrelevant to the life and thought of the average man, he is deliberately saying that Christian dogma, as such, is irrelevant.

But if Christian dogma is irrelevant to life, to what, in Heaven's name, is it relevant? — since religious dogma is in fact nothing but a statement of doctrines concerning the nature of life and the universe. If Christian ministers

---

[25] Dr. W. B. Selbie, "The Army and the Churches," *The Spectator* 164, no. 5823 (2 February 1940): 140.

really believe it is only an intellectual game for theologians and has no bearing upon human life, it is no wonder that their congregations are ignorant, bored, and
bewildered. And indeed, in the very next paragraph Dr.
Selbie recognizes the relation of Christian dogma to life:

> Peace can only happen through a practical appli-
> cation of Christian principles and values. But this
> must have behind it *something more than a reaction
> against* that *Pagan Humanism* which has now been
> found wanting.[26]

The "something else" is dogma, and it cannot be anything else, for between Humanism and Christianity and
between Paganism and Theism there is no distinction
whatever except a distinction of dogma. That you cannot have Christian principles without Christ is becoming increasingly clear, because their validity as principles
depends on Christ's authority; and as we have seen, the
totalitarian states, having ceased to believe in Christ's
authority, are logically quite justified in repudiating
Christian principles. If "the average man" is required
to "believe in Christ" and accept His authority for
"Christian principles," it is surely relevant to inquire

[26] Ibid.

who or what Christ is, and why His authority should
be accepted. But the question, "What think ye of Christ?"
lands the average man at once in the very knottiest kind
of dogmatic riddle. It is quite useless to say that it doesn't
matter particularly who or what Christ was or by what
authority He did those things, and that even if He was
only a man, He was a very nice man and we ought to
live by His principles: for that is merely Humanism, and
if the "average man" in Germany chooses to think that
Hitler is a nicer sort of man with still more attractive
principles, the Christian Humanist has no answer to
make.

It is not true at all that dogma is "hopelessly irrelevant"
to the life and thought of the average man. What is true
is that ministers of the Christian religion often assert that
it is, present it for consideration as though it were, and,
in fact, by their faulty exposition of it make it so. The
central dogma of the Incarnation is that by which relevance stands or falls. If Christ was only man, then He
is entirely irrelevant to any thought about God; if He
is only God, then He is entirely irrelevant to any experience of human life. It is, in the strictest sense, *necessary*
to the salvation of relevance that a man should believe
rightly the Incarnation of our Lord Jesus Christ. Unless
he believes rightly, there is not the faintest reason why he

should believe at all. And in that case, it is wholly irrelevant to chatter about "Christian principles."

If the "average man" is going to be interested in Christ
at all, it is the dogma that will provide the interest. The
trouble is that, in nine cases out of ten, he has never
been offered the dogma. What he has been offered is a
set of technical theological terms which nobody has
taken the trouble to translate into language relevant to
ordinary life.

"Jesus Christ, the Son of God, is God and man." What
does this suggest, except that God the Creator (the irrita-
ble old gentleman with the beard) in some mysterious
manner fathered upon the Virgin Mary something am-
phibious, neither one thing nor t'other, like a merman?
And, like human sons, wholly distinct from and (with
some excuse) probably antagonistic to the father?

And what, in any case, has this remarkable hybrid to
do with John Brown or Tommy Atkins? This attitude of
mind is that called by theologians Nestorianism,[27] or perhaps a debased form of Arianism.[28] But we really cannot

[27] Christian heresy named after Nestorius (d. about 451),
bishop of Constantinople. He taught that there were two
separate persons in Christ, one divine and one human.

[28] Christian heresy named after Arius (c. 250-336), a priest
of Alexandria in Egypt. He denied the full divinity of
Christ.

just give it a technical label and brush it aside as something irrelevant to the thought of the average man. The average man produced it. It is, in fact, an immediate and unsophisticated expression of the thought of the average man. And at the risk of plunging him into the abominable heresy of the Patripassians or the Theopaschites,[29] we must unite with Athanasius[30] to assure Tommy Atkins that the God who lived and died in the world was the same God who created the world, and that, therefore, God Himself has the best possible reasons for understanding and sympathizing with Tommy's personal troubles.

"But," Tommy Atkins and John Brown will instantly object, "it can't have mattered very much to Him if He was God. A god can't really suffer like you and me. Besides, the parson says we are to try and be like Christ; but that's all nonsense — we can't be God, and it's silly to ask us to try." This able exposition of the Eutychian heresy[31] can scarcely be dismissed as merely "interesting to theologians"; it appears to interest Atkins and Brown to the

---

[29] Early Christian heresies that claimed that Christ's divine nature suffered as well as His human nature during the Passion.

[30] Bishop of Alexandria (c. 296-373), opponent of Arius and defender of the Nicene Creed.

[31] Christian heresy named after Eutyches (c. 378-454), a monk from Constantinople. He denied that the human nature of Christ was consubstantial with ours.

point of irritation. Willy-nilly, we are forced to involve ourselves further in dogmatic theology and insist that Christ is "perfect God *and perfect man.*"

At this point, language will trip us up. The average man is not to be restrained from thinking that "perfect God" implies a comparison with gods less perfect, and that "perfect man" means "the best kind of man you can possibly have."

While both these propositions are quite true, they are not precisely what we want to convey. It will perhaps be better to say, "altogether God and altogether man" — God and man at the same time, in every respect and completely; God from eternity to eternity and from the womb to the grave, a man also from the womb to the grave and now.

"That," replies Tommy Atkins, "is all very well, but it leaves me cold. Because, if Jesus was God all the time He must have known that His sufferings and death and so on wouldn't last, and He could have stopped them by a miracle if He had liked, so His pretending to be an ordinary man was nothing but playacting." And John Brown adds, "You can't call a person 'altogether man' if He was God and didn't want to do anything wrong. It was easy enough for Him to be good, but it's not at all the same thing for me. How about all that temptation stuff?

Playacting again. It doesn't help me to live what you call a Christian life."

John and Tommy are now on the way to becoming convinced Apollinarians,[32] a fact which, however "interesting to theologians," has a distinct relevance also to the lives of those average men, since they propose, on the strength of it, to dismiss "Christian principles" as impracticable. There is no help for it. We must insist upon Christ's possession of "a reasonable soul" as well as "human flesh"; we must admit the human limitations of knowledge and intellect; we must take a hint from Christ Himself and suggest that miracles belong to the Son of Man as well as to the Son of God; we must postulate a human will liable to temptation; and we must be quite firm about saying "Equal to the Father as touching His Godhead *and inferior to the Father as touching His Manhood.*" Complicated as the theology is, the average man has walked straight into the heart of the Athanasian Creed, and we are bound to follow.

Teachers and preachers never make it sufficiently clear, I think, that dogmas are not a set of arbitrary regulations invented *a priori* by a committee of theologians

---

[32] Christian heresy named after Apollinarius of Laodicea (c. 310-390). He denied that Christ possessed a rational human soul and thus a full human psychology.

enjoying a bout of all-in dialectical wrestling. Most of
them were hammered out under pressure of urgent practical necessity to provide an answer to heresy.

And heresy is, as I have tried to show, largely the
expression of opinion of the untutored average man, trying to grapple with the problems of the universe at the
point where they begin to interfere with his daily life and
thought. To me, engaged in my diabolical occupation of
going to and fro in the world and walking up and down
in it, conversations and correspondence bring daily a
magnificent crop of all the standard heresies. As practical examples of the "life and thought of the average man"
I am extremely well familiar with them, though I had to
hunt through the encyclopedia to fit them with their
proper theological titles for the purposes of this address.
For the answers I need not go so far: they are compendi-
ously set forth in the Creeds.

But an interesting fact is this: that nine out of ten of
my heretics are exceedingly surprised to learn that the
Creeds contain any statements that bear a practical and
comprehensible meaning. If I tell them it is an article of
faith that the same God who created the world endured
the suffering of the world, they ask in perfect good faith
what connection there is between that statement and the
story of Jesus. If I draw their attention to the dogma that

the same Jesus who was the Divine Love was also Light of Light, the Divine Wisdom, they are surprised. Some of them thank me very heartily for this entirely novel and original interpretation of Scripture, which they never heard of before and suppose me to have invented. Others say irritably that they don't like to think that wisdom and religion have anything to do with one another, and that I should do much better to cut out the wisdom and reason and intelligence and stick to a simple gospel of love. But whether they are pleased or annoyed, they are interested; and the thing which interests them, whether or not they suppose it to be my invention, is the resolute assertion of the dogma.

As regards Dr. Selbie's complaint that insistence on dogma only affronts people and throws into relief the internecine quarrels of Christendom, may I say two things? First, I believe it to be a grave mistake to present Christianity as something charming and popular with no offense in it. Seeing that Christ went about the world giving the most violent offense to all kinds of people, it would seem absurd to expect that the doctrine of His Person can be so presented as to offend nobody. We cannot blink the fact that gentle Jesus meek and mild was so stiff in His opinions and so inflammatory in His language that He was thrown out of church, stoned, hunted from place to place, and finally gibbeted as a firebrand and a public danger. Whatever His peace was, it was not the peace of an amiable indifference; and He said in so many words that what He brought with Him was fire and sword. That being so, nobody need be too much surprised or disconcerted at finding that a determined preaching of Christian dogma may sometimes result in a few angry letters of protest or a difference of opinion on the parish council.

The other thing is this: that I find by experience there is a very large measure of agreement among Christian denominations on all doctrine that is really ecumenical. A rigidly Catholic interpretation of the Creeds, for example — even including the Athanasian Creed — will find support both in Rome and in Geneva. Objections will come chiefly from the heathen, and from a noisy but not very representative bunch of heretical parsons who once in their youth read Robertson[33] or Conybeare[34] and have never gotten over it. But what is urgently necessary is that

---

[33] Probably Frederick W. Robertson (1816-1853), Anglican preacher in the "Broad Church" theological tradition, which objected to positive definition in theology and preferred to interpret Anglican formularies and rubrics in a broad and liberal sense.

[34] Probably Frederick C. Conybeare (1856-1924), an Armenian studies scholar and author of a book on Christian origins, Myth, Magic, and Morals (1909), which attacked Christianity.

certain fundamentals should be restated in terms that make their meaning — and indeed, the mere fact that they have a meaning — clear to the ordinary uninstructed heathen to whom the technical language of theology has become a dead letter.

May I now mention some of the dogmas concerning which I find there is most ignorance and misunderstanding and about which I believe the modern world most urgently needs to be told? Out of a very considerable number I have selected seven as being what I may call "key positions," namely, God, man, sin, judgment, matter, work, and society. They are, of course, all closely bound together — Christian doctrine is not a set of rules, but one vast interlocking rational structure — but there are particular aspects of these seven subjects which seem to me to need special emphasis at the moment.

1. *God.* — At the risk of appearing quite insolently obvious, I shall say that if the Church is to make any impression on the modern mind She will have to preach Christ and the Cross.

Of late years, the Church has not succeeded very well in preaching Christ: She has preached Jesus, which is not quite the same thing. I find that the ordinary man simply does not grasp *at all* the idea that Jesus Christ and God the Creator are held to be literally the same person.

They believe Catholic doctrine to be that God the Father made the world and that Jesus Christ redeemed
mankind, and that these two characters are quite separate personalities.

The phrasing of the Nicene Creed is in this respect a
little unfortunate — it is easy to read it as: "being of one
substance with the-Father-by-whom-all-things-were-made."
The Church Catechism — again rather unfortunately —
emphasizes the distinction: "God the Father, who hath
made me, and all the world. . . . God the Son, who hath
redeemed me, and all mankind."[35] The distinction of the
Persons within unity of the Substance is philosophically
quite proper, and familiar enough to any creative artist:
but the majority of people are not creative artists, and they
have it very firmly fixed in their heads that the Person
who bore the sins of the world was not the eternal creative
life of the world, but an entirely different person, who
was in fact the victim of God the Creator. It is dangerous
to emphasize one aspect of a doctrine at the expense of
the other, but at this present moment the danger that
anybody will confound the Persons is so remote as to
be negligible. What everybody does is to divide the
substance, with the result that the whole Jesus-history

[35] "A Catechism" in *The Book of Common Prayer*, 1928
edition (New York: James Pott and Co., 1929), 570.

becomes an unmeaning anecdote of the brutality of God to man.

It is only with the confident assertion of the creative divinity of the Son that the doctrine of the Incarnation becomes a real revelation of the structure of the world. And here Christianity has its enormous advantage over every other religion in the world. It is the *only* religion which gives value to evil and suffering. It affirms — not, like Christian Science, that evil has no real existence, nor, like Buddhism, that good consists in a refusal to experience evil — but that perfection is attained through the active and positive effort to wrench a real good out of a real evil.

I will not now go into the very difficult question of the nature of evil and the reality of not-being, though the modern physicists seem to be giving us a very valuable lead about that particular philosophic dilemma. But it seems to me most important that, in face of present world conditions, the doctrines of the reality of evil and the value of suffering should be kept in the very front line of Christian affirmation. I mean, it is not enough to say that religion produces virtues and personal consolations side by side with the very obvious evils and pains that afflict mankind, but that God is alive and at work *within* the evil and *within* the suffering, perpetually transforming them by the positive energy which He had with the Father before the world was made.

2. Man. — A young and intelligent priest remarked to me the other day that he thought one of the greatest sources of strength in Christianity today lay in the profoundly pessimistic view it took of human nature. There is a great deal in what he says. The people who are most discouraged and made despondent by the barbarity and stupidity of human behavior at this time are those who think highly of *Homo sapiens* as a product of evolution, and who still cling to an optimistic belief in the civilizing influence of progress and enlightenment. To them, the appalling outbursts of bestial ferocity in the totalitarian states, and the obstinate selfishness and stupid greed of capitalist society, are not merely shocking and alarming. For them, these things are the utter negation of everything in which they have believed. It is as though the bottom had dropped out of their universe. The whole thing looks like a denial of all reason, and they feel as if they and the world had gone mad.

Now for the Christian, this is not the case. He is as deeply shocked and grieved as anybody else, but he is not astonished. He has never thought very highly of human nature left to itself. He has been accustomed to the idea that there is a deep interior dislocation in the very center of human personality, and that you can never, as they say, "make people good by Act of Parliament," because laws are man-made and therefore partake of the imperfect and self-contradictory nature of man. Humanly speaking, it is not true at all that "truly to know the good is to do the good"; it is far truer to say with St. Paul that "the evil which I would not, that I do,"[36] so that the mere increase of knowledge is of very little help in the struggle to outlaw evil.

The delusion of the mechanical perfectibility of man through a combination of scientific knowledge and unconscious evolution has been responsible for much heartbreak. It is, at bottom, far more pessimistic than Christian pessimism, because, if science and progress break down, there is nothing to fall back upon. Humanism is self-contained — it provides for man no resources outside himself.

The Christian dogma of the double nature in man — which asserts that man is disintegrated and necessarily imperfect in himself and in all his works, yet closely related by a real unity of substance with an eternal perfection within and beyond him — makes the present parlous state of human society seem both less hopeless and less irrational. I say "the present parlous state" — but that is

[36] Rom. 7:19.

to limit it too much. A man told me the other day: "I have a little boy of a year old. When the War broke out, I was very much distressed about him, because I found I was taking it for granted that life ought to be better and easier for him than it had been for my generation. Then I realized that I had no right to take this for granted at all — that the fight between good and evil must be the same for him as it had always been, and then I ceased to feel so much distressed."

As Lord David Cecil[37] has said: "The jargon of the philosophy of progress taught us to think that the savage and primitive state of man is behind us; we still talk of the present 'return to barbarism.' But barbarism is not behind us; it is beneath us." And in the same article he observes: "Christianity has compelled the mind of man, not because it is the most cheering view of human existence, but because it is truest to the facts."

I think this is true; and it seems to me quite disastrous that the idea should have got about that Christianity is an otherworldly, unreal, idealistic kind of religion which suggests that if we are good we shall be happy — or if not, it will all be made up to us in the next existence. On the

---

[37] Lord David Cecil (1902-1986), English writer and editor of the *Oxford Book of Christian Verse* (Oxford: Clarendon Press, 1940).

contrary, it is fiercely and even harshly realistic, insisting that the Kingdom of Heaven can never be attained in this world except by unceasing toil and struggle and vigilance: that, in fact, we cannot be good and cannot be happy, but that there are certain eternal achievements that make even happiness look like trash. It has been said, I think by Berdyaev,[38] that nothing can prevent the human soul from preferring creativeness to happiness. In this lies man's substantial likeness to the Divine Christ who in this world suffers and creates continually, being incarnate in the bonds of matter.

3. *Sin.* — This doctrine of man leads naturally to the doctrine of sin. One of the really surprising things about the present bewilderment of humanity is that the Christian Church now finds Herself called upon to proclaim the old and hated doctrine of sin as a gospel of cheer and encouragement. The final tendency of the modern philosophies, which were hailed in their day as a release from the burden of sinfulness, has been to bind man hard and fast in the chains of an iron determinism. The influences of heredity and environment, of glandular make-up and the control exercised by the unconscious, of economic necessity and the mechanics of biological

[38] Nikolai Berdyaev (1874-1948), Russian religious philosopher.

development, have all been invoked to assure man that he is not responsible for his misfortunes and therefore not to be held guilty. Evil has been represented as something imposed upon him from without, not made by him from within.

The dreadful conclusion follows inevitably, that as he is not responsible for evil, he cannot alter it; even though evolution and progress may offer some alleviation in the future, there is no hope for you and me, here and now. I remember well how an aunt of mine, brought up in an old-fashioned liberalism, protested angrily against having continually to call herself a "miserable sinner" when reciting the Litany. Today, if we could really be persuaded that we *are* miserable sinners — that the trouble is not outside us but inside us, and that therefore, by the grace of God, we can do something to put it right — we should receive that message as the most hopeful and heartening thing that one could imagine.

Needless to say, the whole doctrine of "original sin" will have to be restated, in terms which the ordinary modern man, brought up on biology and Freudian psychology, can understand. These sciences have done an enormous amount to expose the *nature* and *mechanism* of man's inner dislocation and ought to be powerful weapons in the hand of the Church. It is a thousand pities that the Church should ever have allowed these weapons to be turned against Her.

4. *Judgment.* — Much the same thing is true of the doctrine of judgment. The word *punishment* for sin has become so corrupted that it ought never to be used. But once we have established the true doctrine of man's nature, the true nature of judgment becomes startlingly clear and rational. It is the inevitable consequence of man's attempt to regulate life and society on a system that runs counter to the facts of his own nature.

In the physical sphere, typhus and cholera are a judgment on dirty living; not because God shows an arbitrary favoritism to nice, clean people, but because of an essential element in the physical structure of the universe. In the State, the brutal denial of freedom to the individual will issue in a judgment of blood, because man is so made that oppression is more intolerable to him than death. The avaricious greed that prompts men to cut down forests for the speedy making of money brings down a judgment of flood and famine, because that sin of avarice in the spiritual sphere runs counter to the physical laws of nature. We must not say that such behavior is wrong because it does not pay; but rather that it does not pay because it is wrong. As T. S. Eliot says, "A wrong attitude towards nature implies, somewhere, a wrong attitude towards God, and the consequence is an inevitable doom."[39]

5. *Matter.* — At this point we shall find ourselves compelled to lay down the Christian doctrine concerning the material universe; and it is here, I think, that we shall have our best opportunity to explain the meaning of sacramentalism. The common man labors under a delusion that for the Christian, matter is evil and the body is evil. For this misapprehension, St. Paul must bear some of the blame, St. Augustine of Hippo a good deal more, and Calvin a very great deal.

But so long as the Church continues to teach the manhood of God and to celebrate the sacraments of the Eucharist and of marriage, no living man should dare to say that matter and body are not sacred to Her. She must insist strongly that the whole material universe is an expression and incarnation of the creative energy of God, as a book or a picture is the material expression of the creative soul of the artist.

For this very reason, all good and creative handling of the material universe is holy and beautiful, and all abuse of the material universe is a crucifixion of the body of Christ. The whole question of the right use to be made

[39] T. S. Eliot, "The Idea of a Christian Society" (New York: Harcourt, Brace and Company, 1940), 62.

of art, of the intellect, and of the material resources of the world is bound up in this. Because of this, the exploitation of man or of matter for commercial uses stands condemned, together with all debasement of the arts and perversions of the intellect.

If matter and the physical nature of man are evil, or if they are of no importance except as they serve an economic system, then there is nothing to restrain us from abusing them as we choose — nothing, except the absolute certainty that any such abuse will eventually come up against the unalterable law and issue in judgment and destruction. In these as in all other matters we cannot escape the law; we have only the choice of fulfilling it freely by the way of grace or willy-nilly by the way of judgment.

6. *Work.* — The unsacramental attitude of modern society to man and matter is probably closely connected with its unsacramental attitude to work.

The Church is a good deal to blame for having connived at this. From the eighteenth century onwards, She has tended to acquiesce in what I call the "industrious apprentice" view of the matter: "Work hard and be thrifty, and God will bless you with a contented mind and a competence." This is nothing but enlightened self-interest in its vulgarest form, and plays directly into the hands of the monopolist and the financier. Nothing has so deeply discredited the Christian Church as Her squalid submission to the economic theory of society. The burning question of the Christian attitude to money is being so eagerly debated nowadays that it is scarcely necessary to do more than remind ourselves that the present unrest, both in Russia and in Central Europe, is an immediate judgment upon a financial system that has subordinated man to economics, and that no *mere* readjustment of economic machinery will have any lasting effect if it keeps man a prisoner inside the machine.

This is the burning question; but I believe there is a still more important and fundamental question waiting to be dealt with, and that is, what men in a Christian Society ought to think and feel about work. Curiously enough, apart from the passage in Genesis which suggests that work is a hardship and a judgment on sin,[40] Christian doctrine is not very explicit about work. I believe, however, that there *is* a Christian doctrine of work, very closely related to the doctrines of the creative energy of God and the divine image in man. The modern tendency seems to be to identify work with gainful employment; and this is, I maintain, the essential heresy at the back of the great economic fallacy which allows wheat and coffee

[40] Gen. 3:17-19.

to be burnt and fish to be used for manure while whole populations stand in need of food. The fallacy being that work is not the expression of man's creative energy in the service of society, but only something he does in order to obtain money and leisure.

A very able surgeon put it to me like this: "What is happening," he said, "is that nobody works for the sake of getting the thing done. The actual result of the work is a by-product; the *aim* of the work is to make money to do something else. Doctors practice medicine, not primarily to relieve suffering, but to make a living — the cure of the patient is something that happens on the way. Lawyers accept briefs, not because they have a passion for justice, but because the law is the profession which enables them to live. The reason," he added, "why men often find themselves happy and satisfied in the army is that for the first time in their lives they find themselves doing something, not for the sake of the pay, which is miserable, but for the sake of getting the thing done."

I will only add to this one thing which seems to me very symptomatic. I was shown a "scheme for a Christian Society" drawn up by a number of young and earnest Roman Catholics. It contained a number of clauses dealing with work and employment — minimum wages, hours of labor, treatment of employees, housing, and so forth — all very proper and Christian. But it offered no machinery whatever for ensuring that the work itself should be properly done. In its lack of a sacramental attitude to work, that is, it was as empty as a set of trade-union regulations. We may remember that a medieval guild did insist, not only on the employer's duty to his workmen, but also on the laborer's duty to his work.

If man's fulfillment of his nature is to be found in the full expression of his divine creativeness, then we urgently need a Christian doctrine of work, which shall provide not only for proper conditions of employment, but also that the work shall be such as a man may do with his whole heart, and that he shall do it for the very work's sake. But we cannot expect a sacramental attitude to work, while many people are forced, by our evil standard of values, to do work which is a spiritual degradation — for example, a long series of financial trickeries or the manufacture of vulgar and useless trivialities.

7. *Society.* — Lastly, a word or two about the Christian doctrine of society — not about its translation into political terms, but about its dogmatic basis. It rests on the doctrine of what God is and what man is, and it is impossible to have a Christian doctrine of society *except* as a corollary to Christian dogma about the place of man in the universe. This is, or should be, obvious.

Creed or Chaos?

The one point to which I should like to draw attention
is the Christian doctrine of the moral law. The attempt to
abolish wars and wickedness by the moral law is doomed
to failure, because of the fact of sinfulness. Law, like every
other product of human activity, shares the integral human
imperfection: it is, in the old Calvinistic phrase, "of the
nature of sin." That is to say: all legality, if erected into
an absolute value, contains within itself the seeds of judgment and catastrophe. The law is necessary, but only, as
it were, as a protective fence against the forces of evil,
behind which the divine activity of grace may do its re-
deeming work. We can, for example, never make a positive peace or a positive righteousness by enactments
against offenders; law is always prohibitive, negative, and
corrupted by the interior contradictions of man's divided
nature; it belongs to the category of judgment. That is
why an intelligent understanding about sin is necessary
to preserve the world from putting an unjustified confi-
dence in the efficacy of the moral law taken by itself. It
will never drive out Beelzebub; it cannot, because it is
only human and not divine.

Nevertheless, the law must be rightly understood or it
is not possible to make the world understand the meaning of grace. There is only one real law — the law of the
universe; it may be fulfilled either by way of judgment or

by way of grace, but it *must* be fulfilled one way or the other. If men will not understand the meaning of judgment, they will never come to understand the meaning of grace. "And [Abraham] said unto him, If they hear not Moses or the Prophets, neither will they be persuaded, though one rose from the dead."[41]

[41] Luke 16:31.

Chapter Five

Strong Meat

"For every one that useth milk is unskillful
in the word of righteousness; for he is a babe.
But strong meat belongeth to them that are of full age,
even those who by reason of use have their senses
exercised to discern both good and evil."

Hebrews 5:13-14

﹃

It is over twenty years since I first read the following words
in some forgotten book. I remember neither the name of
the author, nor that of the saint from whose meditations
he was quoting.[42] Only the statement itself has survived the
accidents of transmission: "*Cibus sum grandium; cresce, et
manducabis me*" — "I am the food of the full-grown; become a man, and thou shalt feed on me."

Here is a robust assertion of the claim of Christianity
to be a religion for adult minds. I am glad to think, now,
that it impressed me so forcibly *then*, when I was still
comparatively young. To protest, when one has left one's
youth behind, against the prevalent assumption that there
is no salvation for the middle-aged is all very well; but it
is apt to provoke a mocking reference to the fox who

---

[42] But I would have laid any odds, from the style, that it was
Augustine of Hippo; and so, indeed, it proves to be (*Con-
fessions*, Bk. 7, ch. 10).

lost his tail. One is in a stronger position if one can show that one had already registered the protest before circumstances rendered it expedient.

There is a popular school of thought (or, more strictly, of feeling) which violently resents the operation of Time upon the human spirit. It looks upon age as something between a crime and an insult. Its prophets have banished from their savage vocabulary all such words as *adult, mature, experienced, venerable;* they know only snarling and sneering epithets, like *middle-aged, elderly, stuffy, senile,* and *decrepit.* With these they flagellate that which they themselves are, or must shortly become, as if abuse were an incantation to exorcize the inexorable. Theirs is neither the thoughtless courage that "makes mouths at the invisible event,"[43] nor the reasoned courage that foresees the event and endures it; still less is it the ecstatic courage that embraces and subdues the event. It is the vicious and desperate fury of a trapped beast; and it is not a pretty sight.

Such men, finding no value for the world as it is, proclaim very loudly their faith in the future, "which is in the hands of the young." With this flattery, they bind their own burden on the shoulders of the next generation. For their own failures, Time alone is to blame — not Sin,

---

[43] William Shakespeare, *Hamlet,* Act 4, scene 4, line 50.

which is expiable, but Time, which is irreparable. From the relentless reality of age they seek escape into a fantasy of youth — their own or other people's. First love, boyhood ideals, childish dreams, the song at the mother's breast, the blind security of the womb — from these they construct a monstrous fabric of pretense, to be their hiding place from the tempest. Their faith is not really in the future, but in the past. Paradoxical as it may seem, to believe in youth is to look backward; to look forward, we must believe in age.

"Except," said Christ, "ye become as little children" — and the words are sometimes quoted to justify the flight into infantilism. Now, children differ in many ways, but they have one thing in common. Peter Pan — if indeed he exists otherwise than in the nostalgic imagination of an adult — is a case for the pathologist. All normal children (however much we discourage them) look forward to growing up. "Except ye become as little children," except you can wake on your fiftieth birthday with the same forward-looking excitement and interest in life that you enjoyed when you were five, "ye cannot see the Kingdom of God."[44] One must not only die daily, but every day one must be born again.

[44] Cf. Matt. 18:3.

Creed or Chaos?

"How can a man be born when he is old?" asked
Nicodemus. His question has been ridiculed; but it is
very reasonable and even profound. "Can he enter a second time into his mother's womb, and be born?"[45] Can
he escape from Time, creep back into the comfortable
prenatal darkness, renounce the values of experience?
The answer makes short work of all such fantasies. "That
which is born of the flesh is flesh; and that which is born
of the Spirit is spirit."[46] The spirit alone is eternal youth;
the mind and the body must learn to make terms with
Time.

Time is a difficult subject for thought, because in a
sense we know too much about it. It is perhaps the only
phenomenon of which we have direct apprehension;
if all our senses were destroyed, we should still remain
aware of duration. Moreover, all conscious thought is a
process in time; so that to think consciously about Time
is like trying to use a foot rule to measure its own length.
The awareness of timelessness, which some people have,
does not belong to the order of conscious thought and
cannot be directly expressed in the language of conscious thought, which is temporal. For every conscious

[45] John 3:4.
[46] John 3:6.

human purpose (including thought) we are compelled to reckon (in every sense of the word) with Time.

Now, the Christian Church has always taken a thoroughly realistic view of Time, and has been very particular to distinguish between Time and Eternity. In Her view of the matter, Time is not an aspect or a fragment of Eternity, nor is Eternity an endless extension of Time; the two concepts belong to different categories. Both have a divine reality: God is the Ancient of Days and also the "I am":[47] the Everlasting, and also the Eternal Present; the *Logos* and also the Father. The Creeds, with their usual practicality, issue a sharp warning that we shall get into a nasty mess if we confuse the two or deny the reality of either. Moreover, the mystics — those rare spirits who are simultaneously aware of both Time and Eternity — support the doctrine by their knowledge and example. They are never vague, woolly-minded people to whom Time means nothing; on the contrary, they insist more than anybody upon the validity of Time and the actuality of human experience.

The reality of Time is not affected by considering it as a dimension in a space-time continuum or as a solid having dimensions of its own. "There's a great devil in

[47] Exod. 3:14.

the universe," says Kay in the play *Time and the Conways*,
"and we call it Time. . . . If things were merely mixed —
good and bad — that would be all right, but they get
worse. . . . Time's beating us."

Her brother replies that Time is "only a kind of dream,"
and that the "happy young Conways of the past" are still
real and existing. "We're seeing another bit of the view —
a bad bit if you like — but the whole landscape's still
there. . . . At this moment, or any moment, we're only a
cross section of our real selves. What we *really* are is the
whole stretch of ourselves, all our time, and when we
come to the end of this life, all our time will be *us* —
the real you, the real me."[48]

Granted all of this — that the happy young Conways still coexist, *now*, with the unhappy, middle-aged
Conways; granted also the converse — that the unhappy,
middle-aged Conways already coexisted, *then*, with the
happy young Conways. What of it? All we have done is
to substitute a spatial image for a temporal one. Instead
of a *progress* from good to evil we have a *prospect* (or
"landscape") of mixed good and evil, which, viewed in
its entirety ("when we come to the end of this life") must
necessarily contain more evil than good, since things "get

---

[48] J. B. Priestley, *Time and the Conways* (Play; 1937), Act 2.

worse and worse." Kay may find this "all right"; the fact remains that there is here no conquest over Time, but an unconditional surrender.

That surrender is made in the moment when we assume that Time is evil in itself and brings nothing but deterioration. It is a pity that the Conway family contained no saint, no artist, no one who had achieved any measure of triumphant fulfillment. His opinion would have been of great interest, since he might have spoken with authority of the soul's development in Time, of the vigorous grappling with evil that transforms it into good, of the dark night of the soul that precedes crucifixion and issues in resurrection.

In contending with the problem of evil it is useless to try to escape either *from* the bad past or *into* the good past. The only way to deal with the past is to accept the *whole* past, and by accepting it, to change its meaning.

The hero of T. S. Eliot's *The Family Reunion*, haunted by the guilt of a hereditary evil, seeks at first "To creep back through the little door"[49] into the shelter of the unaltered past, and finds no refuge there from the pursuing hounds of Heaven. "Now I know / That the last apparent refuge, the safe shelter, / That is where one meets them;

[49] T. S. Eliot, *The Family Reunion*, Part 1, scene 1.

that is the way of specters."[50] So long as he flees from Time and Evil he is in thrall to them; not till he welcomes them does he find strength to transmute them. "And now I know / That my business is not to run away, but to pursue, / Not to avoid being found, but to seek. . . . / It is at once the hardest thing, and the only thing possible. / Now they will lead me. I shall be safe with them; / I am not safe here. . . . / I must follow the bright angels."

Then, and only then, is he enabled to apprehend the good in the evil and to see the terrible hunters of the soul in their true angelic shape. "I feel quite happy, as if happiness / Did not consist in getting what one wanted, / Or in getting rid of what can't be got rid of, / But in a different vision."[51] It is the release, not from, but into, Reality.

This is the great way of Christian acceptance — a very different thing from so-called "Christian" resignation, which merely submits without ecstasy. "Repentance," says a Christian writer, "is no more than a passionate intention to know all things after the mode of Heaven, and it is impossible to know evil as good if you insist on knowing it as evil."[52] For man's evil knowledge, "there could be

---

[50] Ibid., Part 2, scene 2.

[51] Ibid.

[52] Charles Williams, *He Came Down from Heaven* (London: Faber and Faber, 1956), 60.

but one perfect remedy — to know the evil of the past itself as good, and to be free from the necessity of evil in the future — to find right knowledge and perfect freedom together; to know all things as occasions of love."[53]

The story of Passiontide and Easter is the story of the winning of that freedom and of that victory over the evils of Time. The burden of the guilt is accepted ("He was made Sin"[54]), the last agony of alienation from God is passed through ("*Eloi, lama sabachthani*"[55]); the temporal Body is broken and remade; and Time and Eternity are reconciled in a Single Person. There is no retreat here to the Paradise of primal ignorance; the new Kingdom of God is built upon the foundations of spiritual experience. Time is not denied; it is fulfilled. "I am the food of the full-grown."

[53] Ibid., 58.
[54] Cf. 2 Cor. 5:21.
[55] Mark 15:34: "My God, my God, why hast Thou forsaken me?"

Chapter Six

⸎

Why Work?

᳁

I have already, on a previous occasion, spoken at some length on the subject of Work and Vocation.[56] What I urged then was a thoroughgoing revolution in our whole attitude to work. I asked that it should be looked upon, not as a necessary drudgery to be undergone for the purpose of making money, but as a way of life in which the nature of man should find its proper exercise and delight and so fulfill itself to the glory of God. That it should, in fact, be thought of as a creative activity undertaken for the love of the work itself; and that man, made in God's image, should make things, as God makes them, for the sake of doing well a thing that is well worth doing.

[56] These topics were covered in a speech at Brighton in March 1941. The major part of that speech was published in A Christian Basis for the Post-War World (S.C.M. Press). "Why Work?" was first presented as a speech at Eastbourne, England, April 23, 1942.

Creed or Chaos?

It may well seem to you — as it does to some of my acquaintances — that I have a sort of obsession about this business of the right attitude to work. But I do insist upon it, because it seems to me that what becomes of civilization after this war is going to depend enormously on our being able to effect this revolution in our ideas about work. Unless we do change our whole way of thought about work, I do not think we shall ever escape from the appalling squirrel cage of economic confusion in which we have been madly turning for the last three centuries or so, the cage in which we landed ourselves by acquiescing in a social system based upon Envy and Avarice.

A society in which consumption has to be artificially stimulated in order to keep production going is a society founded on trash and waste, and such a society is a house built upon sand.

It is interesting to consider for a moment how our outlook has been forcibly changed for us in the last twelve months by the brutal presence of war. War is a judgment that overtakes societies when they have been living upon ideas that conflict too violently with the laws governing the universe. People who would not revise their ideas voluntarily find themselves compelled to do so by the sheer pressure of the events which these very ideas have served to bring about.

Never think that wars are irrational catastrophes: they happen when wrong ways of thinking and living bring about intolerable situations; and whichever side may be the more outrageous in its aims and the more brutal in its methods, the root causes of conflict are usually to be found in some wrong way of life in which all parties have acquiesced, and for which everybody must, to some extent, bear the blame.

It is quite true that false Economics are one of the root causes of the present war; and one of the false ideas we had about Economics was a false attitude both to Work and to the goods produced by Work. This attitude we are now being obliged to alter, under the compulsion of war — and a very strange and painful process it is in some ways. It is always strange and painful to have to change a habit of mind; though, when we have made the effort, we may find a great relief, even a sense of adventure and delight, in getting rid of the false and returning to the true.

Can you remember   it is already getting difficult to remember — what things were like before the war? The stockings we bought cheap and threw away to save the trouble of mending? The cars we scrapped every year to keep up with the latest fashion in engine design and streamlining? The bread and bones and scraps of fat that littered the dustbins — not only of the rich, but of the poor? The empty bottles that even the dustman scorned to collect, because the manufacturers found it cheaper to make new ones than to clean the old? The mountains of empty tins that nobody found it worthwhile to salvage, rusting and stinking on the refuse dumps? The food that was burnt or buried because it did not pay to distribute it? The land choked and impoverished with thistle and ragwort, because it did not pay to farm it? The handkerchiefs used for paint rags and kettleholders? The electric lights left blazing because it was too much trouble to switch them off? The fresh peas we could not be bothered to shell, and threw aside for something out of a tin? The paper that cumbered the shelves, and lay knee-deep in the parks, and littered the seats of railway trains? The scattered hairpins and smashed crockery, the cheap knickknacks of steel and wood and rubber and glass and tin that we bought to fill in an odd half hour at Woolworth's and forgot as soon as we had bought them? The advertisements imploring and exhorting and cajoling and menacing and bullying us to glut ourselves with things we did not want, in the name of snobbery and idleness and sex appeal? And the fierce international scramble to find in helpless and backward nations a market on which to fob off all the superfluous rubbish which the inexorable machines ground out hour by hour, to create money and to create employment?

Do you realize how we have had to alter our whole scale of values, now that we are no longer being urged to consume but to conserve? We have been forced back to the social morals of our great-grandparents. When a piece of lingerie costs three precious coupons, we have to consider, not merely its glamour value, but how long it will wear. When fats are rationed, we must not throw away scraps, but jealously use to advantage what it cost so much time and trouble to breed and rear. When paper is scarce we must — or we should — think whether what we have to say is worth saying before writing or printing it. When our life depends on the land, we have to pay in short commons for destroying its fertility by neglect or overcropping. When a haul of herrings takes valuable manpower from the forces, and is gathered in at the peril of men's lives by bomb and mine and machine gun, we read a new significance into those gloomy words which appear so often in the fishmonger's shop: NO FISH TODAY. . . . We have had to learn the bitter lesson that in all the world there are only two sources of real wealth: the fruit of the earth and the labor of men; and to estimate work not by the money it brings to the producer, but by the worth of the thing that is made.

Creed or Chaos?

The question that I will ask you to consider today is this: When the war is over, are we likely, and *do we want*, to keep this attitude to work and the results of work? Or are we preparing, and *do we want*, to go back to our old habits of thought? Because I believe that on our answer to this question the whole economic future of society will depend.

Sooner or later the moment will come when we have to make a decision about this. At the moment, we are not making it — don't let us flatter ourselves that we are. It is being made for us. And don't let us imagine that a wartime economy has stopped waste. It has not. It has only transferred it elsewhere. The glut and waste that used to clutter our own dustbins have been removed to the field of battle. That is where all the surplus consumption is going. The factories are roaring more loudly than ever, turning out night and day goods that are of no conceivable value for the maintenance of life; on the contrary, their sole object is to destroy life, and instead of being thrown away they are being blown away — in Russia, in North Africa, over Occupied France, in Burma, China, and the Spice Islands, and on the Seven Seas.

What is going to happen when the factories stop turning out armaments? No nation has yet found a way to keep the machines running and whole nations employed

under modern industrial conditions without wasteful consumption. For a time, a few nations could contrive to
keep going by securing a monopoly of production and
forcing their waste products on to new and untapped
markets. When there are no new markets and all nations
are industrial producers, the only choice we have been
able to envisage so far has been that between armaments
and unemployment. This is the problem that some time
or other will stare us in the face again, and this time we
must have our minds ready to tackle it. It may not come
at once — for it is quite likely that after the war we shall
have to go through a further period of managed consumption while the shortages caused by the war are being made
good. But sooner or later we shall have to grapple with
this difficulty, and everything will depend on our attitude
of mind about it.

Shall we be prepared to take the same attitude to the
arts of peace as to the arts of war? I see no reason why we
should not sacrifice our convenience and our individual
standard of living just as readily for the building of great
public works as for the building of ships and tanks —
but when the stimulus of fear and anger is removed, shall
we be prepared to do any such thing? Or shall we *want* to
go back to that civilization of greed and waste which we
dignify by the name of a "high standard of living"? I am

getting very much afraid of that phrase about the standard of living. And I am also frightened by the phrase "after the war" — it is so often pronounced in a tone that suggests: "after the war, we want to relax, and go back, and live as we did before." And that means going back to the time when labor was valued in terms of its cash returns, and not in terms of the work.

Now the answer to this question, if we are resolute to know what we are about, will not be left to rich men — to manufacturers and financiers. If these people have governed the world of late years it is only because we ourselves put the power into their hands. The question can and should be answered by the worker and the consumer.

It is extremely important that the worker should really understand where the problem lies. It is a matter of brutal fact that in these days labor, more than any other section of the community, has a vested interest in war. Some rich employers make profit out of war — that is true; but what is infinitely more important is that for all working people war means full employment and high wages.

When war ceases, then the problem of employing labor at the machines begins again. The relentless pressure of hungry labor is behind the drive toward wasteful consumption, whether in the destruction of war or in the trumpery of peace.

The problem is far too much simplified when it is
presented as a mere conflict between labor and capital,
between employed and employer. The basic difficulty remains, even when you make the State the sole employer,
even when you make Labor into the employer. It is not
simply a question of profits and wages or living conditions — but of what is to be done with the work of the
machines, and what work the machines are to do.

If we do not deal with this question now, while we
have time to think about it, then the whirligig of wasteful production and wasteful consumption will start again
and will again end in war. And the driving power of labor
will be thrusting to turn the wheels, because it is to the
financial interest of labor to keep the whirligig going
faster and faster till the inevitable catastrophe comes.

And, so that those wheels may turn, the consumer —
that is, you and I, including the workers, who are con-
sumers also — will again be urged to consume and waste,
and unless we change our attitude — or rather unless
we keep hold of the new attitude forced upon us by the
logic of war — we shall again be bamboozled by our vanity, indolence, and greed into keeping the squirrel cage
of wasteful economy turning. We could — you and I —
bring the whole fantastic economy of profitable waste
down to the ground overnight, without legislation and

without revolution, merely by refusing to cooperate with it.
I say, we could — as a matter of fact, we have; or rather,
it has been done for us. If we do not want it to rise up
again after the war, we can prevent it — simply by pre-
serving the wartime habit of valuing work instead of
money. The point is: do we *want* to? . . .

Whatever we do, we shall be faced with grave difficul-
ties. That cannot be disguised. But it will make a great difference to the result if we are genuinely aiming at a real
change in economic thinking. And by that I mean a radi-
cal change from top to bottom — a new system; not a
mere adjustment of the old system to favor a different set
of people.

The habit of thinking about work as something one
does to make money is so ingrained in us that we can
scarcely imagine what a revolutionary change it would be
to think about it instead in terms of the work done. To
do so would mean taking the attitude of mind we reserve
for our unpaid work — our hobbies, our leisure interests,
the things we make and do for pleasure — and making
that the standard of all our judgments about things and
people. We should ask of an enterprise, not "will it pay?"
but "is it good?"; of a man, not "what does he make?" but
"what is his work worth?"; of goods, not "can we induce
people to buy them?" but "are they useful things well

made?"; of employment, not "how much a week?" but
"will it exercise my faculties to the utmost?" And shareholders in — let us say — brewing companies, would
astonish the directorate by arising at shareholders' meetings and demanding to know, not merely where the
profits go or what dividends are to be paid, not even
merely whether the workers' wages are sufficient and
the conditions of labor satisfactory, but loudly and with
a proper sense of personal responsibility: "What goes into
the beer?"

You will probably ask at once: How is this altered attitude going to make any difference to the question of employment? Because it sounds as though it would result in
not more employment, but less. I am not an economist,
and I can only point to a peculiarity of war economy that
usually goes without notice in economic textbooks. In
war, production for wasteful consumption still goes on:
but there is one great difference in the goods produced.
None of them is valued for what it will fetch, but only
for what it is worth in itself. The gun and the tank, the
airplane and the warship have to be the best of their kind.
A war consumer does not buy shoddy. He does not buy to
sell again. He buys the thing that is good for its purpose,
asking nothing of it but that it shall do the job it has to
do. Once again, war forces the consumer into a right

attitude to the work. And, whether by strange coincidence, or whether because of some universal law, as soon as nothing is demanded of the thing made but its own integral perfection, its own absolute value, the skill and labor of the worker are fully employed and likewise acquire an absolute value.

This is probably not the kind of answer that you will find in any theory of economics. But the professional economist is not really trained to answer, or even to ask himself questions about absolute values. The economist is inside the squirrel cage and turning with it. Any question about absolute values belongs to the sphere, not of economics, but of religion.

And it is very possible that we cannot deal with economics at all, unless we can see economy from outside the cage; that we cannot begin to settle the relative values without considering absolute values. And if so, this may give a very precise and practical meaning to the words: "Seek ye first the kingdom of God, and His righteousness; and all these things shall be added to you."[57] . . . I am persuaded that the reason why the Churches are in so much difficulty about giving a lead in the economic sphere is because they are trying to fit a Christian standard of

[57] Matt. 6:33.

economics to a wholly false and pagan understanding of work.

What is the Christian understanding of work? . . . I should like to put before you two or three propositions arising out of the doctrinal position which I stated at the beginning: namely, that work is the natural exercise and function of man — the creature who is made in the image of his Creator. You will find that any one of them, if given in effect everyday practice, is so revolutionary (as compared with the habits of thinking into which we have fallen), as to make all political revolutions look like conformity.

The first, stated quite briefly, is that work is not, primarily, a thing one does to live, but the thing one lives to do. It is, or it should be, the full expression of the worker's faculties, the thing in which he finds spiritual, mental, and bodily satisfaction, and the medium in which he offers himself to God.

Now the consequences of this are not merely that the work should be performed under decent living and working conditions. That is a point we have begun to grasp, and it is a perfectly sound point. But we have tended to concentrate on it to the exclusion of other considerations far more revolutionary.

(a) There is, for instance, the question of profits and remuneration. We have all got it fixed in our heads that the proper end of work is to be paid for — to produce a return in profits or payment to the worker which fully or more than compensates the effort he puts into it. But if our proposition is true, this does not follow at all. So long as Society provides the worker with a sufficient return in real wealth to enable him to carry on the work properly, then he has his reward. For his work is the measure of his life, and his satisfaction is found in the fulfillment of his own nature, and in contemplation of the perfection of his work.

That, in practice, there is this satisfaction, is shown by the mere fact that a man will put loving labor into some hobby which can never bring him any economically adequate return. His satisfaction comes, in the godlike manner, from looking upon what he has made and finding it very good. He is no longer bargaining with his work, but serving it. It is only when work has to be looked on as a means to gain that it becomes hateful; for then, instead of a friend, it becomes an enemy from whom tolls and contributions have to be extracted. What most of us demand from society is that we should always get out of it a little *more* than the value of the labor we give to it. By this process, we persuade ourselves that society is always in our debt — a conviction that not only piles up actual financial burdens, but leaves us with a grudge against society.

(b) Here is the second consequence. At present we have no clear grasp of the principle that every man should do the work for which he is fitted by nature. The employer is obsessed by the notion that he must find cheap labor, and the worker by the notion that the best-paid job is the job for him. Only feebly, inadequately, and spasmodically do we ever attempt to tackle the problem from the other end, and inquire: What type of worker is suited to this type of work? People engaged in education see clearly that this is the right end to start from; but they are frustrated by economic pressure, and by the failure of parents on the one hand and employers on the other to grasp the fundamental importance of this approach. And that the trouble results far more from a failure of intelligence than from economic necessity is seen clearly under war conditions, when, although competitive economics are no longer a governing factor, the right men and women are still persistently thrust into the wrong jobs, through sheer inability on everybody's part to imagine a purely vocational approach to the business of fitting together the worker and his work.

(c) A third consequence is that, if we really believed this proposition and arranged our work and our standard of values accordingly, we should no longer think of work as something that we hastened to get through in order to enjoy our leisure; we should look on our leisure as the period of changed rhythm that refreshed us for the delightful purpose of getting on with our work. And, this being so, we should tolerate no regulations of any sort that prevented us from working as long and as well as our enjoyment of work demanded. We should resent any such restrictions as a monstrous interference with the liberty of the subject. How great an upheaval of our ideas that would mean I leave you to imagine. It would turn topsy-turvy all our notions about hours of work, rates of work, unfair competition, and all the rest of it. We should all find ourselves fighting, as now only artists and the members of certain professions fight, for precious time in which to get on with the job — instead of fighting for precious hours saved from the job.

(d) A fourth consequence is that we should fight tooth and nail, not for mere employment, but for the quality of the work that we had to do. We should clamor to be engaged in work that was worth doing, and in which we could take pride. The worker would demand that the stuff he helped to turn out should be good stuff — he would no longer be content to take the cash and let the credit go. Like the shareholders in the brewery, he would feel a sense of personal responsibility, and clamor to know, and to control, what went into the beer he brewed. There

would be protests and strikes — not only about pay and
conditions, but about the quality of the work demanded
and the honesty, beauty, and usefulness of the goods produced. The greatest insult which a commercial age has
offered to the worker has been to rob him of all interest
in the end product of the work and to force him to dedi-
cate his life to making badly things which were not worth
making.

This first proposition chiefly concerns the worker as
such. My second proposition directly concerns Christians
as such, and it is this: It is the business of the Church to
recognize that the secular vocation, as such, is sacred.
Christian people, and particularly perhaps the Christian
clergy, must get it firmly into their heads that when a man
or woman is called to a particular job of secular work, that
is as true a vocation as though he or she were called to
specifically religious work. The Church must concern
Herself not only with such questions as the just price
and proper working conditions: She must concern Herself with seeing that the work itself is such as a human
being can perform without degradation — that no one is
required by economic or any other considerations to de-
vote himself to work that is contemptible, soul destroying, or harmful. It is not right for Her to acquiesce in the
notion that a man's life is divided into the time he spends

on his work and the time he spends in serving God. He must be able to serve God in his work, and the work itself must be accepted and respected as the medium of divine creation.

In nothing has the Church so lost Her hold on reality as in Her failure to understand and respect the secular vocation. She has allowed work and religion to become separate departments, and is astonished to find that, as a result, the secular work of the world is turned to purely selfish and destructive ends, and that the greater part of the world's intelligent workers have become irreligious, or at least, uninterested in religion.

But is it astonishing? How can any one remain interested in a religion which seems to have no concern with nine-tenths of his life? The Church's approach to an intelligent carpenter is usually confined to exhorting him not to be drunk and disorderly in his leisure hours, and to come to church on Sundays. What the Church *should* be telling him is this: that the very first demand that his religion makes upon him is that he should make good tables.

Church by all means, and decent forms of amusement, certainly — but what use is all that if in the very center of his life and occupation he is insulting God with bad carpentry? No crooked table legs or ill-fitting drawers ever, I dare swear, came out of the carpenter's shop at Nazareth. Nor, if they did, could anyone believe that they were made by the same hand that made Heaven and earth. No piety in the worker will compensate for work that is not true to itself; for any work that is untrue to its own technique is a living lie.

Yet in Her own buildings, in Her own ecclesiastical art and music, in Her hymns and prayers, in Her sermons and in Her little books of devotion, the Church will tolerate or permit a pious intention to excuse work so ugly, so pretentious, so tawdry and twaddling, so insincere and insipid, so *bad* as to shock and horrify any decent draftsman.

And why? Simply because She has lost all sense of the fact that the living and eternal truth is expressed in work only so far as that work is true in itself, to itself, to the standards of its own technique. She has forgotten that the secular vocation is sacred. Forgotten that a building must be good architecture before it can be a good church; that a painting must be well painted before it can be a good sacred picture; that work must be good work before it can call itself God's work.

Let the Church remember this: that every maker and worker is called to serve God *in* his profession or trade — not outside it. The Apostles complained rightly when they said it was not meet they should leave the word of

God and serve tables; their vocation was to preach the word.[58] But the person whose vocation it is to prepare the meals beautifully might with equal justice protest: It is not meet for us to leave the service of our tables to preach the word.

The official Church wastes time and energy, and, moreover, commits sacrilege, in demanding that secular workers should neglect their proper vocation in order to do Christian work — by which She means ecclesiastical work. The only Christian work is good work well done. Let the Church see to it that the workers are Christian people and do their work well, as to God: then all the work will be Christian work, whether it is church embroidery, or sewage farming. As Jacques Maritain says: "If you want to produce Christian work, be a Christian, and try to make a work of beauty into which you have put your heart; do not adopt a Christian pose."[59] He is right. And let the Church remember that the beauty of the work will be judged by its own, and not by ecclesiastical standards.

Let me give you an illustration of what I mean. When my play *The Zeal of Thy House* was produced in London,

---

[58] Acts 6:2.

[59] Ch. 8, "Christian Art," sect. 2, in Jacques Maritain, *Art and Scholasticism with Other Essays*, trans. J. F. Scanlon (New York: Charles Scribner's Sons, 1930), 70.

a dear old pious lady was much struck by the beauty of
the four great archangels who stood throughout the play
in their heavy, gold robes, eleven feet high from wingtip
to sandaltip. She asked with great innocence whether
I selected the actors who played the angels "for the excellence of their moral character."

I replied that the angels were selected, to begin with,
not by me but by the producer, who had the technical qualifications for selecting suitable actors — for that was part
of his vocation. And that he selected, in the first place,
young men who were six feet tall so that they would match
properly together. Secondly, angels had to be of good phy-
sique, so as to be able to stand stiff on the stage for two and
a half hours, carrying the weight of their wings and cos-
tumes, without wobbling, or fidgeting, or fainting. Thirdly,
they had to be able to speak verse well, in an agreeable
voice and audibly. Fourthly, they had to be reasonably
good actors. When all these technical conditions had been
fulfilled, we might come to the moral qualities, of which
the first would be the ability to arrive on the stage punc-
tually and in a sober condition, since the curtain must go
up on time, and a drunken angel would be indecorous.

After that, and only after that, one might take character into consideration, but that, provided his behavior
was not so scandalous as to cause dissension among the

company, the right kind of actor with no morals would give a far more reverent and seemly performance than a saintly actor with the wrong technical qualifications. The worst religious films I ever saw were produced by a company which chose its staff exclusively for their piety. Bad photography, bad acting, and bad dialogue produced a result so grotesquely irreverent that the pictures could not have been shown in churches without bringing Christianity into contempt.

God is not served by technical incompetence; and incompetence and untruth always result when the secular vocation is treated as a thing alien to religion. . . .

And conversely: when you find a man who is a Christian praising God by the excellence of his work — do not distract him and take him away from his proper vocation to address religious meetings and open church bazaars. Let him serve God in the way to which God has called him. If you take him away from that, he will exhaust himself in an alien technique and lose his capacity to do his dedicated work. It is your business, you churchmen, to get what good you can from observing his work — not to take him away from it, so that he may do ecclesiastical work for you. But, if you have any power, see that he is set free to do his own work as well as it may be done. He is not there to serve you; he is there to serve God by serving his work.

This brings me to my third proposition; and this may sound to you the most revolutionary of all. It is this: the worker's first duty is to *serve the work*. The popular catchphrase of today is that it is everybody's duty to serve the community. It is a well-sounding phrase, but there *is* a catch in it. It is the old catch about the two great commandments. "Love God — and your neighbor; on those two commandments hang all the Law and the Prophets."[60]

The catch in it, which nowadays the world has largely forgotten, is that the second commandment depends upon the first, and that without the first, it is a delusion and a snare. Much of our present trouble and disillusionment have come from putting the second commandment before the first.

If we put our neighbor first, we are putting man above God, and that is what we have been doing ever since we began to worship humanity and make man the measure of all things. Whenever man is made the center of things, he becomes the storm center of trouble — and that is precisely the catch about serving the community. It ought perhaps to make us suspicious of that phrase when we consider that it is the slogan of every commercial

[60] Cf. Matt. 22:37-40.

scoundrel and swindler who wants to make sharp business practice pass muster as social improvement.

"Service" is the motto of the advertiser, of big business, and of fraudulent finance. And of others, too. Listen to this: "I expect the judiciary to understand that the nation does not exist for their convenience, but that justice exists to serve the nation." That was Hitler yesterday — and that is what becomes of "service," when the community, and not the work, becomes its idol. There is, in fact, a paradox about working to serve the community, and it is this: that to aim directly at serving the community is to falsify the work; the only way to serve the community is to forget the community and serve the work. There are three very good reasons for this:

The first is that you cannot do good work if you take your mind off the work to see how the community is taking it — any more than you can make a good drive from the tee if you take your eye off the ball. "Blessed are the singlehearted" (for that is the real meaning of the word we translate "the pure in heart"[61]). If your heart is not wholly in the work, the work will not be good — and work that is not good serves neither God nor the community; it only serves mammon.

[61] Matt. 5:8.

The second reason is that the moment you think
of serving other people, you begin to have a notion that
other people owe you something for your pains; you begin
to think that you have a claim on the community. You
will begin to bargain for reward, to angle for applause,
and to harbor a grievance if you are not appreciated. But
if your mind is set upon serving the work, then you know
you have nothing to look for; the only reward the work
can give you is the satisfaction of beholding its perfection.
The *work* takes all and gives nothing but itself; and to
serve the work is a labor of pure love.

And thirdly, if you set out to serve the community, you
will probably end by merely fulfilling a public demand —
and you may not even do that. A public demand is a
changeable thing. Nine-tenths of the bad plays put on
in theaters owe their badness to the fact that the playwright has aimed at pleasing the audience, instead of at
producing a good and satisfactory play. Instead of doing
the work as its own integrity demands that it should be
done, he has falsified the play by putting in this or that
which he thinks will appeal to the groundlings[62] (who by

---

[62] An English slang term that originally referred to specta-
tors in the cheapest seats in a theater. It came to refer to
"those of ordinary or unsophisticated taste or critical
judgment."

that time have probably come to want something else), and the play fails by its insincerity. The work has been falsified to please the public, and in the end even the public is not pleased. As it is with works of art, so it is with all work.

We are coming to the end of an era of civilization which began by pandering to public demand, and ended by frantically trying to create public demand for an output so false and meaningless that even a doped public revolted from the trash offered to it and plunged into war rather than swallow any more of it. The danger of "serving the community" is that one is part of the community, and that in serving it one may only be serving a kind of communal egotism.

The only true way of serving the community is to be truly in sympathy with the community, to be oneself part of the community, and then to serve the work, without giving the community another thought. Then the work will endure, because it will be true to itself. It is the work that serves the community; the business of the worker is to serve the work.

Where we have become confused is in mixing up the *ends* to which our work is put with the *way* in which the work is done. The end of the work will be decided by our religious outlook: as we *are* so we *make*. It is the business of religion to make us Christian people, and then our work will naturally be turned to Christian ends, because our work is the expression of ourselves. But the way in which the work is done is governed by no sanction except the good of the work itself; and religion has no direct connection with that, except to insist that the workman should be free to do his work well according to its own integrity. Jacques Maritain, one of the very few religious writers of our time who really understand the nature of creative work, has summed the matter up in a sentence:

> What is required is the perfect practical discrimination between the end pursued by the workman (*finis operantis*, said the Schoolmen) and the end to be served by the work (*finis operis*), so that the workman may work for his wages but the work be controlled and set in being only in relation to its own proper good and nowise in relation to the wages earned; so that the artist may work for any and every human intention he likes, but the work taken by itself be performed and constructed for its own proper beauty alone.[63]

[63] Ch. 9, "Art and Morality," sect. 2, in Maritain, *Art and Scholasticism*, 77-78.

Creed or Chaos?

Or perhaps we may put it more shortly still: If work is to find its right place in the world, it is the duty of the Church to see to it that the work serves God, and that the worker serves the work.

Chapter Seven

૪

The Other Six Deadly Sins

⚛

Perhaps the bitterest commentary on the way in which
Christian doctrine has been taught in the last few centuries is the fact that to the majority of people the word
immorality has come to mean one thing and one thing
only.[64]

The name of an association like yours is generally
held to imply that you are concerned to correct only one
sin out of those seven which the Church recognizes as
capital. By a hideous irony, our shrinking reprobation of
that sin has made us too delicate so much as to name it,
so that we have come to use for it the words which were
made to cover the whole range of human corruption.

A man may be greedy and selfish; spiteful, cruel, jealous, and unjust; violent and brutal; grasping, unscrupulous,
and a liar; stubborn and arrogant; stupid, morose, and

[64] This is the text of an address delivered at Westminster,
England, October 23, 1941.

dead to every noble instinct — and still we are ready to say of him that he is not an immoral man. I am reminded of a young man who once said to me with perfect simplicity: "I did not know there were seven deadly sins: please tell me the names of the other six."

About the sin called *Luxuria* or Lust, I shall therefore say only three things. First, that it is a sin, and that it ought to be called plainly by its own name, and neither huddled away under a generic term like *immorality*, nor confused with love.

Secondly, that up till now the Church, in hunting down this sin, has had the active alliance of Caesar, who has been concerned to maintain family solidarity and the orderly devolution of property in the interests of the State. But now that contract and not status is held to be the basis of society, Caesar need no longer rely on the family to maintain social solidarity; and now that so much property is held anonymously by trusts and joint-stock companies, the laws of inheritance lose a great deal of their importance. Consequently, Caesar is now much less interested than he was in the sleeping arrangements of his citizens, and has in this matter cynically denounced his alliance with the Church. This is a warning against putting one's trust in any child of man — particularly in Caesar. If the Church is to continue Her campaign against Lust, She must do so on her own — that is, on sacramental — grounds; and she will have to do it, if not in defiance of Caesar, at least without his assistance.

Thirdly, there are two main reasons for which people fall into the sin of *Luxuria*. It may be through sheer exuberance of animal spirits: in which case a sharp application of the curb may be all that is needed to bring the body into subjection and remind it of its proper place in the scheme of man's twofold nature. Or — and this commonly happens in periods of disillusionment like our own, when philosophies are bankrupt and life appears without hope — men and women may turn to lust in sheer boredom and discontent, trying to find in it some stimulus which is not provided by the drab discomfort of their mental and physical surroundings. When *that* is the case, stern rebukes and restrictions are worse than useless. It is as though one were to endeavor to cure anemia by bleeding; it only reduces further an already impoverished vitality. The mournful and medical aspect of twentieth-century pornography and promiscuity strongly suggests that we have reached one of these periods of spiritual depression, where people go to bed because they have nothing better to do. In other words, the "regrettable moral laxity" of which respectable people complain may have its root cause not in *Luxuria* at all, but in some other of the sins of society, and may automatically begin to cure itself when that root cause is removed.

The Church, then, officially recognizes six other capital or basic sins — seven altogether. Of these, three may be roughly called the warm-hearted or disreputable sins, and the remaining four the cold-hearted or respectable sins.

It is interesting to notice that Christ rebuked the three disreputable sins only in mild or general terms, but uttered the most violent vituperations against the respectable ones. Caesar and the Pharisees, on the other hand, strongly dislike anything warm-hearted or disreputable, and set great store by the cold-hearted and respectable sins, which they are in a conspiracy to call virtues. And we may note that, as a result of this unholy alliance between worldly interest and religious opinion, the common man is rather inclined to canonize the warm-hearted sins for himself, and to thank God openly that he is broad-minded, given to a high standard of living, and instinct with righteous indignation — not prurient, straitlaced or namby-pamby, or even as this Pharisee. It is difficult to blame the common man very much for this natural reaction against the insistent identification of Christian morality with everything that Christ most fervently abhorred.

The sin of *Ira* or Wrath is one, perhaps, to which the English as a nation are not greatly addicted, except in a rather specialized form. On the whole we are slow to anger, and dislike violence. We can be brutal and destructive — usually, however, only under provocation; and much of our apparent brutality is due much less to violence of temper than to sheer unimaginative stupidity (a detestable sin in itself, but quite different in nature and origin). On the whole, we are an easygoing, good-humored people, who hate with difficulty and find it almost impossible to cherish rancor or revenge.

This is true, I think, of the English. It is perhaps not quite true of those who profess and call themselves British. The Celt is quarrelsome; he prides himself that with him it is a word and a blow. He broods upon the memory of ancient wrongs in a way that to the Englishman is incomprehensible; if the English were Irish by temperament they would still be roused to fury by the name of the Battle of Hastings, instead of summing it up philosophically as "1066 and All That."

The Celt clings fiercely to his ancient tribal savageries, and his religious habits are disputatious, polemical, and (in extreme instances, as on the Irish border) disgraced by bloodthirst and a persecuting frenzy. But let the Englishman not be in too great a hurry to congratulate himself. He has one besetting weakness, by means of which he may very readily be led or lashed into the sin of Wrath: he is peculiarly liable to attacks of righteous indignation. While he is in one of these fits he will fling himself into a debauch of fury and commit extravagances that are not only evil but ridiculous.

We all know pretty well the man — or perhaps still more frequently the woman — who says that anybody who tortures a helpless animal should be flogged till he shrieks for mercy. The harsh, grating tone and the squinting, vicious countenance accompanying the declaration are enough to warn us that this righteous anger is devil-born, and trembling on the verge of mania. But we do not always recognize this ugly form of possession when it cloaks itself under a zeal for efficiency or a lofty resolution to expose scandals — particularly if it expresses itself only in print or in platform verbiage.

It is very well known to the more unscrupulous part of the Press that nothing pays so well in the newspaper world as the manufacture of schism and the exploitation of wrath. Turn over the pages of the more popular papers if you want to see how avarice thrives on hatred and the passion of violence. To foment grievance and to set men at variance is the trade by which agitators thrive and journalists make money. A dogfight, a brawl, or a war is always news; if news of that kind is lacking, it pays well to contrive it. The average English mind is a fertile field in which to sow the dragon's teeth of moral indignation; and the fight that follows will be blind, brutal, and merciless.

That is not to say that scandals should not be exposed, or that no anger is justified. But you may know the mischief-maker by the warped malignancy of his language as easily as by the warped malignancy of his face and voice. His fury is without restraint and without magnanimity — and it is aimed, not at checking the offense, but at starting a pogrom against the offender. He would rather the evil were not cured at all than that it were cured quietly and without violence. His evil lust of wrath cannot be sated unless somebody is hounded down, beaten, and trampled on, and a savage war dance executed upon the body.

I have said that the English are readily tempted into this kind of debauch. I will add that it *is* a debauch, and, like other debauches, leaves him with a splitting head, a bad hangover, and a crushing sense of shame. When he does give way to wrath, he makes a very degrading exhibition of himself, because wrath is a thing unnatural to him; it affects him like drink or drugs. In the shamefaced mood that follows, he becomes spiritless, sick at heart,

and enfeebled in judgment. I am therefore the more concerned about a highly unpleasant spirit of vindictiveness
that is being commended to us at this moment, camou-
flaged as righteous wrath and a warlike spirit. It is not a
warlike spirit at all — at any rate, it is very unlike the
spirit in which soldiers make war. The good soldier is on
the whole remarkable both for severity in his measures,
and for measure in his severity. He is as bloodthirsty as
his duty requires him to be, and, as a rule, not more. Even
in Germany, the difference between the professional and
the political fighter is said to be very marked in this
respect.

There are, however, certain people here whose mar-
tial howls do not suggest the battle cry even of a savage
warrior so much as Miss Henrietta Petowker reciting
The Blood-Drinker's Burial in Mrs. Kenwigs's front parlor.
If I say: "Do not listen to them," it is not because there
is no room for indignation, but because there is a point
at which righteous indignation passes over into the
deadly sin of Wrath; and once it has passed that point,
it is liable, like all other passions, to stagger over into
its own opposite, the equally fatal sin of Sloth or *Acedia,*
of which we shall have something to say presently.
Ungovernable rage is the sin of the warm heart and
the quick spirit; in such men it is usually very quickly

repented of — though before that happens it may have wrought irreparable destruction. We shall have to see to it that the habit of wrath and destruction which war fastens upon us is not carried over into the peace. And above all we must see to it *now* that our blind rages are not harnessed and driven by those men of the cold head and the cold heart — the Envious, the Avaricious, and the Proud.

The third warm-hearted sin is named *Gula* in Latin and in English, Gluttony. In its vulgarest and most obvious form we may feel that we are not much tempted to it. Certain other classes of people — not ourselves — do, of course, indulge in this disreputable kind of wallowing. Poor people of coarse and unrefined habits drink too much beer. Rich people, particularly in America and in those luxury hotels which we cannot afford, stuff themselves with food. Young people especially girls younger than ourselves — drink far too many cocktails and smoke like chimneys. And some very reprehensible people contrive, even in wartime, to make pigs of themselves in defiance of the rationing order, like the young woman who (according to a recent gossip column) contrived to eat five separate lunches in five separate restaurants in the course of a single morning. But on the whole, England in wartime is not a place where the majority of us can very easily destroy our souls with Gluttony. We may congratulate ourselves that, if we have not exactly renounced our sins, this particular sin at any rate has renounced us.

Let us seize this breathing space, while we are out of reach of temptation, to look at one very remarkable aspect of the sin of *Gula*. We have all become aware lately of something very disquieting about what we call our economic system. An odd change has come over us since the arrival of the machine age. Whereas formerly it was considered a virtue to be thrifty and content with one's lot, it is now considered to be the mark of a progressive nation that it is filled with hustling, go-getting citizens, intent on raising their standard of living. And this is not interpreted to mean merely that a decent sufficiency of food, clothes, and shelter is attainable by all citizens. It means much more and much less than this. It means that every citizen is encouraged to consider more, and more complicated, luxuries necessary to his well-being. The gluttonous consumption of manufactured goods had become, before the war, the prime civic virtue. And why? Because the machines can produce cheaply only if they produce in vast quantities; because unless the machines can produce cheaply nobody can afford to keep them running; and because, unless they are kept running, millions of citizens will be thrown out of employment, and the community will starve.

We need not stop now to go round and round the vicious circle of production and consumption. We need not remind ourselves of the furious barrage of advertisement by which people are flattered and frightened out of a reasonable contentment into a greedy hankering after goods which they do not really need; nor point out for the thousandth time how every evil passion — snobbery, laziness, vanity, concupiscence, ignorance, greed — is appealed to in these campaigns. Nor how unassuming communities (described as "backward countries") have these desires ruthlessly forced upon them by their neighbors in the effort to find an outlet for goods whose market is saturated. And we must not take up too much time in pointing out how, as the necessity to sell goods in quantity becomes more desperate, the people's appreciation of quality is violently discouraged and suppressed.

You must not buy goods that last too long, for production cannot be kept going unless the goods wear out, or fall out of fashion, and so can be thrown away and replaced with others. If a man invents anything that would give lasting satisfaction, his invention must be bought up by the manufacturer so that it may never see the light of day.

Creed or Chaos?

Nor must the worker be encouraged to take too much interest in the thing he makes; if he did, he might desire to make it as well as it can be made, and that would not pay. It is better that he should work in a soulless indifference, even though such treatment should break his spirit, and cause him to hate his work. The difference between the factory hand and the craftsman is that the craftsman lives to do the work he loves; but the factory hand lives by doing the work he despises. The service of the machine will not have it otherwise. We know about all this, and must not discuss it now — but I will ask you to remember it.

The point I want to make *now* is this: that whether or not it is desirable to keep up this fearful whirligig of industrial finance based on gluttonous consumption, it could not be kept up for a single moment without the cooperative gluttony of the consumer. Legislation, the control of wages and profits, the balancing of exports and imports, elaborate schemes for the distribution of surplus commodities, the State ownership of enterprise, complicated systems of social credit, and finally wars and revolutions are all invoked in the hope of breaking down the thing known as the present Economic System.

Now it may well be that its breakdown would be a terrific disaster and produce a worse chaos than that which went before — we need not argue about it. The point is that, without any legislation whatever, the whole system would come crashing down in a day if every consumer were voluntarily to restrict his purchases to the things he really needed. "The fact is," said a working man the other day at a meeting, "that when we fall for these advertisements we're being had for mugs." So we are. The sin of Gluttony, of Greed, of overmuch stuffing of ourselves, is the sin that has delivered us over into the power of the machine.

In evil days between the wars we were confronted with some ugly contrasts between plenty and poverty. Those contrasts should be, and must be, reduced. But let us say frankly that they are not likely to be reduced, so long as the poor admire the rich for the indulgence in precisely that gluttonous way of living which rivets on the world the chain of the present economic system, and do their best to imitate rich men's worst vices. To do that is to play into the hands of those whose interest it is to keep the system going.

You will notice that, under a war economy, the contrast is being flattened out; we are being forced to reduce and regulate our personal consumption of commodities, and to revise our whole notion of what constitutes good citizenship in the financial sense. This is the judgment of this world: when we will not amend ourselves by Grace, we are compelled under the yoke of Law.

You will notice also that we are learning certain things. There seems, for example, to be no noticeable diminution in our health and spirits due to the fact that we have only the choice of, say, half a dozen dishes in a restaurant instead of forty. In the matter of clothing, we are beginning to regain our respect for stuffs that will wear well; we can no longer be led away by the specious argument that it is smarter and more hygienic to wear underlinen and stockings once and then throw them away than to buy things that will serve us for years.

We are having to learn, painfully, to save food and material and to salvage waste products; and in learning to do these things we have found a curious and stimulating sense of adventure. For it is the great curse of Gluttony that it ends by destroying all sense of the precious, the unique, the irreplaceable.

But what will happen to us when the war machine ceases to consume our surplus products for us? Shall we hold fast to our rediscovered sense of real values and our adventurous attitude of life? If so, we shall revolutionize world economy without any political revolution. Or shall we again allow our Gluttony to become the instrument of an economic system that is satisfactory to nobody?

That system as we know it thrives upon waste and rubbish heaps. At present the waste (that is, sheer gluttonous consumption) is being done for us in the field of war. In peace, if we do not revise our ideas, we shall ourselves become its instruments. The rubbish heap will again be piled on our own doorsteps, on our own backs, in our own bellies. Instead of the wasteful consumption of trucks and tanks, metal and explosives, we shall have back the wasteful consumption of wireless sets and silk stockings, drugs and paper, cheap pottery and cosmetics — all the slop and swill that pour down the sewers over which the palace of Gluttony is built.

Gluttony is warm-hearted. It is the excess and perversion of that free, careless, and generous mood which desires to enjoy life and to see others enjoy it. But, like Lust and Wrath, it is a headless, heedless sin, which puts the good-natured person at the mercy of the cold head and the cold heart; and these exploit it and bring it to judgment, so that at length it issues in its own opposite — in that very "dearth in the midst of plenty" at which we stand horrified today.

In particular, it is at the mercy of the sin called *Avaritia* or Covetousness. At one time this sin was content to call itself "Honest Thrift," and under that name was, as they say in Aberdeen, "varra weel respectit." The cold-hearted sins recommend themselves to Church and State by the restraints they lay upon the vulgar and disreputable warm-hearted sins. The thrifty poor do not swill beer in pubs, or indulge in noisy quarrels in the streets to the annoyance of decent people — moreover, they are less likely to become a burden on the rates. The thrifty well-to-do do not abash their pious neighbors by extravagant indulgence in *Gula* or *Luxuria* — which are both very expensive sins. Nevertheless, there used always to be certain reservations about the respect accorded to Covetousness. It was an unromantic, unspectacular sin. Unkind people sometimes called it by rude names, such as *Parsimony* and *Niggardliness*. It was a narrow, creeping, pinched kind of sin; and it was not a good mixer. It was more popular with Caesar than with Caesar's subjects; it had no glamour about it.

It was left for the present age to endow Covetousness with glamour on a big scale, and to give it a title which it could carry like a flag. It occurred to somebody to call it "Enterprise." From the moment of that happy inspiration, Covetousness has gone forward and never looked back. It has become a swaggering, swashbuckling, piratical sin, going about with its hat cocked over its eye, and with pistols tucked into the tops of its jackboots. Its war cries are "Business Efficiency!" "Free Competition!" "Get

Out or Get Under!" and "There's Always Room at the Top!" It no longer screws and saves — it launches out into new enterprises; it gambles and speculates; it thinks in a big way; it takes risks. It can no longer be troubled to deal in real wealth, and so remain attached to Work and the Soil. It has set money free from all such hampering ties; it has interests in every continent; it is impossible to pin it down to any one place or any concrete commodity — it is an adventurer, a roving, rollicking free lance.

It looks so jolly and jovial, and has such a twinkle in its cunning eye, that nobody can believe that its heart is as cold and calculating as ever. Besides, where is its heart? Covetousness is not incarnated in individual people, but in business corporations, joint-stock companies, amalgamations, and trusts, which have neither bodies to be kicked, nor souls to be damned — nor hearts to be appealed to, either: it is very difficult to fasten on anybody the responsibility for the things that are done with money. Of course, if Covetousness miscalculates and some big financier comes crashing down, bringing all the small speculators down with him, we wag self-righteous heads, and feel that we see clearly where the fault lies. But we do not punish the fraudulent businessman for his frauds, but for his failure.

Creed or Chaos?

The Church says Covetousness is a deadly sin — but does She really think so? Is She ready to found Welfare Societies to deal with financial immorality as She does with sexual immorality? Do the officials stationed at church doors in Italy to exclude women with bare arms turn anybody away on the grounds that they are too well dressed to be honest? Do the vigilance committees who complain of "suggestive" books and plays make any attempt to suppress the literature which "suggests" that getting on in the world is the chief object in life? Is Dives,[65] like Magdalen, ever refused the sacraments on the grounds that he, like her, is an "open and notorious evil-liver"? Does the Church arrange services with bright congregational singing, for Total Abstainers from Usury?

The Church's record is not, in these matters, quite as good as it might be. But is perhaps rather better than that of those who denounce Her for Her neglect. The Church is not the Vatican, nor the Metropolitans, nor the Bench of Bishops; it is not even the Vicar or the Curate or the Churchwardens: the Church is you and I. And are you and I in the least sincere in our pretense that we disapprove of Covetousness?

[65] Luke 16:19-31.

Let us ask ourselves one or two questions. Do we admire and envy rich people because they are rich, or because the work by which they made their money is good work? If we hear that Old So-and-so has pulled off a pretty smart deal with the Town Council, are we shocked by the revelation of the cunning graft involved, or do we say admiringly: "Old So-and-so's hot stuff — you won't find many flies on him"? When we go to the cinema and see a picture about empty-headed people in luxurious surroundings, do we say: "What drivel!" or do we sit in a misty dream, wishing we could give up our daily work and marry into surroundings like that? When we invest our money, do we ask ourselves whether the enterprise represents anything useful, or merely whether it is a safe thing that returns a good dividend? Do we regularly put money into football pools or dog racing? When we read the newspaper, are our eyes immediately arrested by anything which says "millions" in large capitals, preceded by the £ or $ sign? Have we ever refused money on the grounds that the work that we had to do for it was something that we could not do honestly, or do well? Do we *never* choose our acquaintances with the idea that they are useful people to know, or keep in with people in the hope that there is something to be got out of them? And do we — this is important — when we blame the mess that the

Creed or Chaos?

economical world has got into, do we always lay the
blame on wicked financiers, wicked profiteers, wicked
capitalists, wicked employers, wicked bankers — or do
we sometimes ask ourselves how far *we* have contributed
to make the mess?

Just as the sin of Gluttony thrives on little greeds, so
the sin of Covetousness thrives on little acts of avarice —
on the stupid and irresponsible small shareholder, for example, who is out to get money for nothing. There is a
book entitled *Wall Street Under Oath*[66] which makes
entertaining but rather shameful reading. It is an account
of the exposure of various great business and banking
frauds in the United States at the time of the postwar
slump. When we have finished wondering at the bare-
faced venality, graspingness, and lack of scruple of the
notorious financiers who stood in the dock to answer the
charge of fraud, we may fruitfully wonder at the incredi-
ble avarice and criminal folly of their victims. For no
share-pusher could vend his worthless stock, if he could
not count on meeting, in his prospective victim, an
unscrupulous avarice as vicious as his own, but stupider.
Every time a man expects, as he says, his money to work
for him, he is expecting other people to work for him; and

[66] Louis Pecora, *Wall Street Under Oath* (New York: Simon &
Schuster, 1939; London: Cresset Press, 1939).

when he expects it to bring in more money in a year than honest work could produce in that time, he is expecting it to cheat and steal on his behalf.

We are all in it together. I often wonder why Germany was so foolishly impatient as to go to war. If domination was all she wanted, she could have it without shedding a drop of blood, by merely waiting long enough and trusting to the avarice of mankind. You may remember the sordid and cynical French businessman on the boat that brought Elie J. Bois to England after the collapse of France. Someone asked him: "Why did France break down like this?" and he answered: "Because she had too many men like me." France was bought — the politicians were bought, the Press was bought, Labor was bought, the Church was bought, big business was bought, even the army was bought. Not always by open bribes in cash, but by the insidious appeal to security, and business interests and economic power.

Nobody would destroy anything or let go of anything; there was always the hope of making a deal with the enemy. Everybody, down to the smallest provincial official and the pettiest petty shopkeeper had a vested interest in nonresistance. Wars are not made by businessmen, who are terrified of the threat to their powers: what businessmen make are surrenders.

Nobody prays more fervently than the businessman to be freed from the "crushing burden of armaments"; the first thing that happens in a war is the freezing of international credits, which the businessman does not like. The same businessman who will view with perfect indifference the senseless destruction of fish and fruit, coffee and corn in peacetime, because it does not pay to distribute them, is preternaturally sensitive about the senseless destruction of property by war. Patience, cunning, and the appeal to avarice could bring the whole world into economic subjection by a slow interior corruption. We may, perhaps, count ourselves fortunate that Hitler's patience was at length exhausted and that he conjured up the devil of Wrath to cast out the devil of Covetousness. When Satan casts out Satan, his kingdom does not stand;[67] but we have come to a grievous pass if we have to choose between one devil and another, if the only deliverance from Covetousness is the Wrath of war, and the only safeguard against war, a peace based on Covetousness.

The virtue of which Covetousness is the perversion is something more positive and warm-hearted than Thrift — it is the love of the real values, of which the material world

[67] Cf. Matt. 12:26.

has only two: the fruits of the earth and the labor of the people. As for the spiritual values, Avarice has no use for them: they cannot be assessed in money, and the moment that anyone tries to assess them in money they softly and suddenly vanish away.

We may argue eloquently that "Honesty is the best policy." Unfortunately, the moment honesty is adopted for the sake of policy it mysteriously ceases to be honesty. We may say that the best Art should be recompensed at the highest rate, and no doubt it should; but if the artist lets his work be influenced by considerations of marketing, he will discover that what he is producing is not Art. And we may say, with some justice, that an irreligious nation cannot prosper; but if a nation tries to cultivate religion for the sake of regaining prosperity, the resulting brand of religion will be addressed to a very queer God indeed. There is said to be a revival just now of what is called "interest" in religion. Even governments are inclined to allot broadcasting time to religious propaganda, and to order National Days of Prayer. However admirable these activities may be, one has a haunting feeling that God's acquaintance is being cultivated because He might come in useful. But God is quite shrewd enough to see through that particular kind of commercial fraud.

But we are only halfway through our list of the Deadly
Sins. Hand in hand with Covetousness goes its close com-
panion — *Invidia* or Envy, which hates to see other men
happy. The names by which it offers itself to the world's
applause are *Right* and *Justice,* and it makes a great parade
of these austere virtues. It begins by asking, plausibly:
"Why should not I enjoy what others enjoy?" and it ends
by demanding: "Why should others enjoy what I may
not?" Envy is the great leveller: if it cannot level things
up, it will level them down; and the words constantly
in its mouth are: "My Rights" and "My Wrongs." At its
best, Envy is a climber and a snob; at its worst, it is a de-
stroyer — rather than have anybody happier than itself,
it will see us all miserable together.

In love, Envy is cruel, jealous, and possessive. My
friend and my married partner must be wholly wrapped
up in me, and must find no interests outside me. That is
my right. No person, no work, no hobby must rob me of
any part of that right. If we cannot be happy together, we
will be unhappy together — but there must be no escape
into pleasures that I cannot share. If my husband's work
means more to him than I do, I will see him ruined rather
than preoccupied; if my wife is so abandoned as to enjoy
Beethoven or dancing, or anything else which I do not
appreciate, I will so nag and insult her that she will no

longer be able to indulge these tastes with a mind at ease.
If my neighbors are able to take pleasure in intellectual
interests which are above my head, I will sneer at them
and call them by derisive names, because they make me
feel inferior, and that is a thing I cannot bear. All men
have equal rights — and if these people were born with
any sort of privilege, I will see to it that that privilege
shall be made worthless — if I can, and by any means I
can devise. Let justice be done to me, though the heav-
ens fall and the earth be shot to pieces.

If Avarice is the sin of the Haves against the Have-
nots, Envy is the sin of the Have-nots against the Haves.
If we want to see what they look like on a big scale,
we may say that Avarice has been the sin of the Anglo-
Saxon democracies, and Envy the sin of Germany. Both
are cruel — the one with a heavy, complacent, and blood-
less cruelty; the other with a violent, calculated, and savage cruelty. But Germany only displays in accentuated
form an evil of which we have plenty at home.

The difficulty about dealing with Envy is precisely that
it *is* the sin of the Have-nots, and that, on that account,
it can always find support among those who are just and
generous-minded. Its demands for a place in the sun are
highly plausible, and those who detect any egotism in
the demand can readily be silenced by accusing them of

oppression, inertia, and a readiness to grind the face of the poor. Let us look for a moment at some of the means by which Envy holds the world to ransom.

One of its achievements has been to change the former order by which society was based on status and substitute a new basis — that of contract. Status means, roughly speaking, that the relations of social units are ordered according to the intrinsic qualities which those units possess by nature. Men and institutions are valued for what they are. Contract means that they are valued, and their relations ordered, in virtue of what bargain they are able to strike. Knowledge, for example, and the man of knowledge, can be rated at a market value — prized, that is, not for the sake of knowledge, but for what is called their contribution to society. The family is esteemed, or not esteemed, according as it can show its value as an economic unit. Thus, all inequalities can, theoretically, be reduced to financial and utilitarian terms, and the very notion of intrinsic superiority can be denied and derided. In other words, all pretension to superiority can be debunked.

The years between the wars saw the most ruthless campaign of debunking ever undertaken by nominally civilized nations. Great artists were debunked by disclosures of their private weaknesses; great statesmen, by attributing to them mercenary and petty motives, or by alleging that all their work was meaningless, or done for them by other people. Religion was debunked, and shown to consist of a mixture of craven superstition and greed. Courage was debunked, patriotism was debunked, learning and art were debunked, love was debunked, and with it family affection and the virtues of obedience, veneration, and solidarity. Age was debunked by youth and youth by age. Psychologists stripped bare the pretensions of reason and self-control and conscience, saying that these were only the respectable disguises of unmentionable unconscious impulses. Honor was debunked with peculiar virulence, and good faith, and unselfishness. Everything that could possibly be held to constitute an essential superiority had the garments of honor torn from its back and was cast out into the darkness of derision. Civilization was finally debunked till it had not a rag left to cover its nakedness.

It is well that the hypocrisies which breed like mushrooms in the shadow of great virtues should be discovered and removed; but Envy is not the right instrument for that purpose; for it tears down the whole fabric to get at the parasitic growths. In fact, virtues themselves are the enemy of envy. Envy cannot bear to admire or respect; it cannot bear to be grateful. But it is very plausible; it always announces that it works in the name of truth and equity.

Sometimes it may be a good thing to debunk Envy a little. For example: here is a phrase which we have heard a good deal of late: "These services (payments, compensations, or what not) ought not to be made a matter of charity. We have a right to demand that they should be borne by the State."

It sounds splendid; but what does it mean?

Now, you and I are the State; and where the bearing of financial burdens is concerned, the taxpayer is the State. The heaviest burden of taxation is, naturally, borne by those who can best afford to pay. When a new burden is imposed, the rich will have to pay most of it.

Of the money expended in charity, the greater part, for obvious reasons, is contributed by the rich. Consequently, if the burden hitherto borne by charity is transferred to the shoulders of the taxpayer, it will inevitably continue to be carried by exactly the same class of people. The only difference is this: that people will no longer pay because they want to — eagerly and for love — but because they must, reluctantly and under pain of fine or imprisonment. The result, roughly speaking, is financially the same: the only difference is the elimination of the two detested virtues of love and gratitude.

I do not say for a moment that certain things should not be the responsibility of the State — that is, of everybody. No doubt those who formerly contributed out of love should be very willing to pay a tax instead. But what I see very clearly is the hatred of the gracious act, and the determination that nobody shall be allowed any kind of spontaneous pleasure in well-doing if Envy can prevent it. "This ointment might have been sold for much and given to the poor."[68] Then our nostrils would not be offended by any odor of sanctity — the house would not be "filled with the smell of the ointment."[69] It is characteristic that it should have been Judas who debunked that act of charity.[70]

[68] Cf. John 12:5.

[69] John 12:3.

[70] It will be noticed that appeasement of Envy is becoming quite an important factor in our domestic war policy. Thus, certain restrictions on hotel and restaurant catering have been imposed, *admittedly*, not because they make any major difference to the nation's food resources but in the name of equality and sacrifice. So far, so good. Similarly, people with large cellars have been debarred from laying in stocks of coal during the summer, *although*, had this been permitted up to the limit of their allocation, the problem of winter delivery would have been greatly eased for the coal merchants, and the people with small cellars would have stood a better chance of getting their coal regularly. So far, perhaps, not quite so good. The controversy about education has been enlivened by a beautiful three-cornered duel. One party thinks the public boarding school so evil a luxury that it ought not to be inflicted even upon the rich. A second party thinks it so desirable a luxury that it ought to be thrown open to the poor. The levellers-up

Creed or Chaos?

The Church names the sixth Deadly Sin *Acedia* or Sloth. In the world it calls itself *Tolerance*; but in Hell it is called *Despair*. It is the accomplice of the other sins and their worst punishment. It is the sin which believes in nothing, cares for nothing, seeks to know nothing, interferes with nothing, enjoys nothing, loves nothing, hates nothing, finds purpose in nothing, lives for nothing, and only remains alive because there is nothing it would die for. We have known it far too well for many years. The only thing perhaps that we have not known about it is that it is mortal sin.

The war has jerked us pretty sharply into consciousness about this slugabed sin of Sloth, and perhaps we say too much about it. But two warnings are rather necessary.

First, it is one of the favorite tricks of this Sin to dissemble itself under cover of a whiffling activity of body.

and the levellers-down are thus embarrassed by a trifling uncertainty as to which is up and which is down; while a third party contends that the whole boarding system bears so hardly on parent and child alike that the poor would not like it if they had it, although they are not sure whether this argues in the poor a laudable love of family life or a lamentable lack of discipline. The only possible comment seems to be that (a) no exercise is so hard and exacting as that of settling a case on its merits (hence the popular dislike of casuistry); (b) it is always easier to level down than to level up; and (c) a distinguished poet has warned us that: "The last temptation is the greatest treason: To do the right deed for the wrong reason." T. S. Eliot, *Murder in the Cathedral*, part 1.

We think that if we are busily rushing about and doing things, we cannot be suffering from Sloth. And besides, violent activity seems to offer an escape from the horrors of Sloth. So the other sins hasten to provide a cloak for Sloth: Gluttony offers a whirl of dancing, dining, sports, and dashing very fast from place to place to gape at beauty spots; which when we get to them, we defile with vulgarity and waste. Covetousness rakes us out of bed at an early hour, in order that we may put pep and hustle into our business; Envy sets us to gossip and scandal, to writing cantankerous letters to the papers, and to the unearthing of secrets and the scavenging of dustbins; Wrath provides (very ingeniously) the argument that the only fitting ac- tivity in a world so full of evil-doers and evil demons is to curse loudly and incessantly "Whatever brute and black- guard made the world"; while Lust provides that round of dreary promiscuity that passes for bodily vigor. But these are all disguises for the empty heart and the empty brain and the empty soul of *Acedia*.

Let us take particular notice of the empty brain. Here Sloth is in a conspiracy with Envy to prevent people from thinking. Sloth persuades us that stupidity is not our sin, but our misfortune; while Envy at the same time persuades us that intelligence is despicable — a dusty, highbrow, and commercially useless thing.

And secondly, the War has jerked us out of Sloth; but wars, if they go on very long, induce Sloth in the shape of war-weariness and despair of any purpose. We saw its effects in the last peace, when it brought all the sins in its train. There are times when one is tempted to say that the great, sprawling, lethargic sin of Sloth is the oldest and greatest of the sins and the parent of all the rest.

But the head and origin of all sin is the basic sin of *Superbia* or Pride. In one way there is so much to say about Pride that one might speak of it for a week and not have done. Yet in another way, all there is to be said about it can be said in a single sentence. It is the sin of trying to be as God. It is the sin which proclaims that Man can produce out of his own wits and his own impulses and his own imagination the standards by which he lives: that Man is fitted to be his own judge. It is Pride which turns man's virtues into deadly sins, by causing each self-sufficient virtue to issue in its own opposite, and as a grotesque and horrible travesty of itself. The name under which Pride walks the world at this moment is the *Perfectibility of Man*, or the *Doctrine of Progress*; and its speciality is the making of blueprints for Utopia and establishing the Kingdom of Man on earth.

For the devilish strategy of Pride is that it attacks us, not on our weak points, but on our strong. It is pre-eminently the sin of the noble mind — that *corruptio optimi*[71] which works more evil in the world than all the deliberate vices. Because we do not recognize pride when we see it, we stand aghast to see the havoc wrought by the triumphs of human idealism. We meant so well, we thought we were succeeding, and look what has come of our efforts! There is a proverb that says that the way to Hell is paved with good intentions. We usually take it as referring to intentions that have been weakly abandoned; but it has a deeper and much subtler meaning. For that road is paved with good intentions strongly and obstinately pursued, until they have become self-sufficing ends in themselves and deified. "Sin grows with doing good. . . . / Servant of God has chance of greater sin / And sorrow, than the man who serves a king. / For those who serve the greater cause may make the cause serve them, / Still doing right."[72]

The Greeks feared above all things the state of mind they called *hubris* — the inflated spirits that come with too much success. Overweening in men called forth, they thought, the envy of the gods. Their theology may seem to us a little unworthy, but with the phenomenon itself and its effects they were only too well acquainted.

---

[71] "Corruption of the best."
[72] T. S. Eliot, *Murder in the Cathedral*, part 1.

Creed or Chaos?

Christianity, with a more rational theology, traces *hubris* back to the root sin of Pride, which places man instead of God at the center of gravity and so throws the whole structure of things into the ruin called Judgment. Whenever we say, whether in the personal, political, or social sphere, "I am the master of my fate, / I am the captain of my soul,"[73] we are committing the sin of Pride; and the higher the goal at which we aim, the more far-reaching will be the subsequent disaster. That is why we ought to distrust all those high ambitions and lofty ideals which make the well-being of humanity their ultimate end. Man cannot make himself happy by serving himself — not even when he calls self-service the service of the community; for "the community" in that context is only an extension of his own ego. Happiness is a by-product, thrown off in man's service of God. And incidentally, let us be very careful how we preach that "Christianity is necessary for the building of a free and prosperous postwar world." The proposition is strictly true, but to put it that way may be misleading, for it sounds as though we proposed to make God an instrument in the service of man. But God is nobody's instrument. If we say that the denial of God was the cause of our present disasters, well and good;

[73] William Ernest Henley (1849-1903), "*Invictus, In Memoriam* R. T. Hamilton Bruce," stanza 4.

it is of the essence of Pride to suppose that we can do without God.

But it will not do to let the same sin creep back in a subtler and more virtuous-seeking form by suggesting that the service of God is necessary as a means to the service of man. That is a blasphemous hypocrisy, which ends by degrading God to the status of a heathen fetish, bound to the service of a tribe, and liable to be dumped head downward in the water butt if He failed to produce good harvest weather in return for services rendered.

"*Cursed be he that trusteth in man*," says theologian Reinhold Niebuhr, "even if he be pious man or, perhaps, particularly if he be pious man."[74] For the besetting temptation of the pious man is to become the proud man: "He spake this parable unto certain which trusted in themselves that they were righteous."[75]

My Lord Bishop, Ladies and Gentlemen, it has been my privilege to suggest to you that in your work for the Moral Welfare of this nation you will be doing a great thing if you can persuade the people that the Church is actively and anxiously concerned not with one kind of

---

[74] Reinhold Niebuhr, *Beyond Tragedy: Essays on the Interpretation of Christian History* (New York: Charles Scribner's Sons, 1955), 124.

[75] Luke 18:9.

sin alone, but with seven sins, all of which are deadly, and not least with those which Caesar sanctions and of which the world approves. And moreover, that whatever disguise the sins assume, the Church knows the right names for all of them. And just in case there is anybody who (like the young man I mentioned) has not the list at his fingertips, let us recite those names again:

Luxuria or Lust,

Ira or Wrath,

Gula or Gluttony,

Avaritia or Covetousness,

Invidia or Envy,

Acedia or Sloth,

Superbia or Pride:

The Seven Deadly Sins.

Biographical Note

⤫

Dorothy L. Sayers

(1893-1957)

❦

Born in Oxford, England, in 1893, Dorothy Sayers was educated privately, and in 1912 entered Somerville College at Oxford University. A member of the first class of women to be awarded degrees at the University, she graduated with first-class honors in French.

In the early 1920s, after a period working in teaching and publishing, Sayers began a career as an advertising copywriter, during which she was responsible for a very successful national campaign for Colman's mustard. Around the same time, the first of her world-famous "Lord Peter Wimsey" detective novels was published. All told, Sayers published twelve detective novels between 1923 and 1937, several of which have become international classics of the genre and are still read and beloved by millions of readers.

Sayers began writing about theological issues in the late 1930s, when she was asked to write a play for the

Canterbury Festival of 1937. The play she wrote, *The Zeal of Thy House*, was followed by a series of BBC radio plays entitled *The Man Born to Be King*. In the 1940s, she wrote numerous other religious essays and books, including *Begin Here*, *The Mind of the Maker*, and *Creed or Chaos?* These writings established Sayers as one of the foremost Christian apologists of her generation.

Sayers's reputation for erudition combined with literary wit and style was further confirmed in the late 1940s and in the 1950s by the publication of her translations of Dante's *Divine Comedy* and *The Song of Roland* for the Penguin Classics.

Novelist, playwright, scholar, and an associate of C. S. Lewis, T. S. Eliot, and Charles Williams, Dorothy Sayers argued passionately for the relevance of orthodox Christian doctrine to the living of a truly Christian life. To the delight of readers everywhere, she did so in terms that were at once uncompromising, learned, and humorous.

The Apostles' Creed

I believe in God, the Father almighty,
creator of Heaven and earth.
I believe in Jesus Christ, His only Son, our Lord.
He was conceived by the power of the Holy Spirit
and born of the Virgin Mary.
He suffered under Pontius Pilate, was crucified,
died, and was buried. He descended into Hell.
On the third day He rose again.
He ascended into Heaven and is seated
at the right hand of the Father.
He will come again to judge the living and the dead.
I believe in the Holy Spirit, the holy catholic Church,
the communion of saints, the forgiveness of sins,
the resurrection of the body,and life everlasting.

The Nicene Creed

We believe in one God, the Father, the Almighty,
maker of Heaven and earth, of all that is, seen and unseen.
We believe in one Lord, Jesus Christ, the only Son of God,
eternally begotten of the Father, God from God,
Light from Light, true God from true God,
begotten, not made, one in Being with the Father.
Through Him all things were made.
For us men and for our salvation He came
down from Heaven: by the power of the Holy
Spirit He was born of the Virgin Mary,
and became man. For our sake He was crucified under
Pontius Pilate; He suffered, died, and was buried.
On the third day He rose again in fulfillment
of the Scriptures; He ascended into Heaven and is seated
at the right hand of the Father. He will come again
in glory to judge the living and the dead,

and His kingdom will have no end.
We believe in the Holy Spirit, the Lord, the giver of life,
who proceeds from the Father and the Son.
With the Father and the Son He is worshipped and glorified.
He has spoken through the Prophets.
We believe in one holy catholic and apostolic Church.
We acknowledge one baptism for the forgiveness of sins.
We look for the resurrection of the dead
and the life of the world to come.

The Athanasian Creed

Whosoever will be saved, before all things it is necessary that he hold the Catholic Faith. Which Faith except everyone do keep whole and undefiled, without doubt he shall perish everlastingly.

And the Catholic Faith is this: That we worship one God in Trinity, and Trinity in Unity, neither confounding the Persons, nor dividing the Substance. For there is one Person of the Father, another of the Son, and another of the Holy Ghost. But the God-head of the Father, of the Son, and of the Holy Ghost is all one, the Glory equal, the Majesty co-eternal. Such as the Father is, such is the Son, and such is the Holy Ghost. The Father uncreate, the Son uncreate, and the Holy Ghost uncreate. The Father incomprehensible, the Son incomprehensible, and the Holy Ghost incomprehensible. The Father eternal, the Son eternal, and the Holy Ghost eternal. And yet they are not three eternals, but one eternal. As also there are not three incomprehensibles, nor three uncreated, but one uncreated, and one incomprehensible. So likewise the Father is Almighty, the Son Almighty, and the Holy Ghost Almighty. And yet they are not three Almighties, but one Almighty. So the Father is God, the Son is God, and the Holy Ghost is God.

And yet they are not three Gods, but one God. So likewise the Father is Lord, the Son Lord, and the Holy Ghost Lord. And yet not three Lords, but one Lord. For like as we are compelled by the

Christian verity to acknowledge every Person by Himself to be
both God and Lord, so are we forbidden by the Catholic Religion,
to say, There be three Gods, or three Lords. The Father is made
of none, neither created, nor begotten. The Son is of the Father
alone, not made, nor created, but begotten. The Holy Ghost is
of the Father and of the Son, neither made, nor created, nor begotten, but proceeding. So there is one Father, not three Fathers;
one Son, not three Sons; one Holy Ghost, not three Holy Ghosts.
And in this Trinity none is afore, or after other; none is greater,
or less than another; But the whole three Persons are co-eternal
together and co-equal. So that in all things, as is aforesaid, the
Unity in Trinity and the Trinity in Unity is to be worshipped.
He therefore that will be saved must thus think of the Trinity.

[handwritten margin note: The Son submitted to the Father not because the Father was greater, but out of love.]

Furthermore, it is necessary to everlasting salvation that he
also believe rightly the Incarnation of our Lord Jesus Christ. For
the right Faith is: that we believe and confess that our Lord Jesus
Christ, the Son of God, is God and Man; God, of the Substance of
the Father, begotten before the worlds; and Man, of the Substance
of His Mother, born in the world; perfect God and perfect Man, of
a reasonable soul and human flesh subsisting; equal to the Father,
as touching His Godhead; and inferior to the Father, as touching
His Manhood. Who although He be God and Man, yet He is not
two, but one Christ; one, not by conversion of the Godhead into
flesh, but by taking of the Manhood into God: One altogether;
not by confusion of Substance, but by unity of Person. For as the
reasonable soul and flesh is one man, so God and Man is one Christ;
who suffered for our salvation, descended into Hell, rose again the
third day from the dead. He ascended into Heaven, He sitteth on
the right hand of the Father, God Almighty, from whence He shall
come to judge the quick and the dead. At whose coming all men
shall rise again with their bodies and shall give account for their
own works. And they that have done good shall go into life everlasting; and they that have done evil into everlasting fire.

[handwritten margin note: whether to submit to the crucifixion or not was a matter concerning his manhood. Therefore, he did the will of his Father]

This is the Catholic Faith, which except a man believe faith-
fully, he cannot be saved.

Sophia Institute Press®

Sophia Institute is a nonprofit institution that seeks to restore man's knowledge of eternal truth, including man's knowledge of his own nature, his relation to other persons, and his relation to God. Sophia Institute Press® serves this end in numerous ways: it publishes translations of foreign works to make them accessible for the first time to English-speaking readers; it brings out-of-print books back into print; and it publishes important new books that fulfill the ideals of Sophia Institute. These books afford readers a rich source of the enduring wisdom of mankind.

Sophia Institute Press® makes these high-quality books available to the general public by using advanced technology and by soliciting donations to subsidize its general publishing costs. Your generosity can help Sophia Institute Press® to provide the public with editions of works containing the enduring wisdom of the ages. Please send your tax-deductible contribution to the address below. We also welcome your questions, comments, and suggestions.

For your free catalog, call:
Toll-free: 1-800-888-9344

or write:
Sophia Institute Press®
Box 5284, Manchester, NH 03108

or visit our website:
www.sophiainstitute.com

Sophia Institute is a tax-exempt institution as defined by the Internal Revenue Code, Section 501(c)(3). Tax I.D. 22-2548708.